a SAVOR THE SOUTH® *cookbook*

Chicken

SAVOR THE SOUTH® *cookbooks*

a SAVOR THE SOUTH® *cookbook*

Chicken

CYNTHIA GRAUBART

The University of North Carolina Press CHAPEL HILL

© 2016 The University of North Carolina Press
All rights reserved. Manufactured in the United States of America.
SAVOR THE SOUTH® is a registered trademark of the
University of North Carolina Press, Inc.
Designed by Kimberly Bryant and set in Miller and
Calluna Sans types by Rebecca Evans.

Jacket illustration: © istockphoto.com/suriyasilsaksom

Library of Congress Cataloging-in-Publication Data
Names: Graubart, Cynthia Stevens, author.
Title: Chicken / Cynthia Graubart.
Other titles: Savor the South cookbook.
Description: Chapel Hill : The University of
North Carolina Press, [2016] |
Series: Savor the South cookbook | Includes index.
Identifiers: LCCN 2016014540| ISBN 9781469630090
(cloth : alk. paper) | ISBN 9781469630106 (ebook)
Subjects: LCSH: Cooking (Chicken) | Cooking, American—Southern style.
Classification: LCC TX750.5.C45 G694 2016 | DDC 641.6/65—dc23
LC record available at https://lccn.loc.gov/2016014540

Catherine Fliegel, this one's for you.

Contents

A Bird in the Hand 123

COOKED CHICKEN ON HAND SAVES THE DAY

SIDEBARS

a SAVOR THE SOUTH® *cookbook*

Chicken

Introduction

"Possibly no other region of the country knows more chicken recipes than the South."

—*John Martin Taylor,* The New Southern Cook

Chicken and Me

One of my earliest memories of chicken is five-year-old me standing outside a white clapboard house in a long line of people waiting to get inside. The heat was oppressive, and I wiggled my sweaty little hand out of my mother's grasp. No one seemed to mind standing in line, and I suppose I didn't either (except for the hand-holding part). The fried chicken served at Beach Road Chicken Dinners on Atlantic Boulevard in Jacksonville, Florida, was worth the wait. All the chicken dinners came with mashed potatoes and creamed peas, and that was the extent of the menu. (I cannot attest to how the peas tasted. It was the only table at which I ever sat for dinner that I was permitted to omit the peas from my plate.) The mashed potatoes were fluffy and gloriously buttery, but I was still allowed to put more pats of butter on top. The chicken arrived so hot that I was the last one at the table who could bite into it. My mom would reach over and lift a little piece of skin, letting the steam escape so maybe I wouldn't have to wait too long. It seems like it was always hot weather when we went to eat there, and, in hindsight, I now suppose that my grandmother, who made wonderful fried chicken herself, had declared it too hot to fry in her own kitchen (no air-conditioning), so we went and ate the second best.

Both grandmothers were good cooks but completely different kinds. Nana, who lived in Jacksonville, had a repertoire of salad- and luncheon-type dishes she produced for her bridge club. Nana Stuffie (short for "short stuff") was a born country cook—she hailed from Hastings, Florida—who grew up wringing chicken necks. And, boy, she could fry chicken! I'm sorry I didn't get her recipes. I'm sorry I never had the chance to spend much time in

1

the kitchen with either one of them. My mother was the queen of can-of-soup casseroles in every suburb we ever lived in, and I didn't want to inherit that crown. I've always said I learned to cook in self-defense.

My college days encouraged my own exploration of new foods and tastes, and not long after graduating, I was producing Nathalie Dupree's nationally syndicated PBS cooking show *New Southern Cooking*. I had no idea there was such a thing as cooking technique—nor that it could be learned. I had always been a good student, and now I saw I could save myself from my unfortunate culinary childhood.

Born in Florida to southern parents and grandparents, I've eaten chicken through my southern lens in the Middle East, South Africa, all over Europe, and in most of these United States. Superior recipes come from every corner of the world, but the ones from your own family or community are the most cherished.

As children, my sister and I couldn't wait for the wishbone to dry on the kitchen windowsill after a meal of whole roast chicken. We believed in the folk wisdom that said that if two people make a wish and pull on opposite ends of the wishbone until it breaks, the wish of the person with the longer end will come true. The pony never arrived, in case you are curious.

I remember when I was twelve years old languishing for three weeks with a horrific bout of the flu, which seemed to last three months in my young mind, and finally having an appetite after an eternity of clear liquids. My mother roasted a chicken sprinkled with a bit of Lawry's seasoned salt (ubiquitous at the time) and served the golden bird with tender green beans and creamy whipped potatoes, both lavished with butter. I still remember the miracle of my reawakened taste buds and appetite that night, and the knowing reassurance that I would indeed live. That menu still reigns supreme as my comfort-food meal of choice.

The Southern Chicken

Chicken is among the most iconic foods in the South, and our connections to it run deep. True southern fried chicken is the chicken dish many dream of long after they've left the South. Sunday dinner here has always been a special meal, and if the preacher was coming, there would surely be chicken on the menu, demonstrating the family's largess in serving a precious dish. Prior to the 1940s, chicken was more expensive than beef or pork. Families with chickens in the yard were reluctant to kill their egg-laying hens, though by the time those hens finished their usefulness as layers, they were tough old birds, fit only for stew.

In the post–World War II South, chicken farming became industrialized, lowering the price, and you could buy chicken nearly everywhere. The poultry industry hit the jackpot when high cholesterol was linked with heart disease. Red meat consumption dropped, and chicken, which is low in cholesterol, was declared a healthier protein. As the popularity of chicken grew, it became a staple for family meals. As distribution widened, there seemed to be "a chicken in every pot."

In what began as a "servistation" in 1930 in Corbin, Kentucky, Colonel Harland Sanders built a motel and restaurant on his gas station property and turned the fried chicken from his restaurant into a franchise known the world over. He invented the process of frying his chicken in large pressure cookers and controlled his secret recipe of eleven herbs and spices by packaging and selling the seasoning mixture to Kentucky Fried Chicken franchisees, never parting with the recipe. The colonel helped to make fried chicken a national dish.

But southerners have strong ideas about fried chicken and what makes the best fried chicken. In 1985, the legendary chef Bill Neal wrote in his acclaimed book *Southern Cooking*, "Southern fried chicken is the center of more controversies than perhaps any other item of food." Frying in lard, shortening, or oil; cooking in a cast-iron skillet or not; and even the flouring method—dry-wet-dry or just dry—are all points of great debate. Do you pat your chicken in flour only once? Or do you then dip it in an egg wash and flour again?

Brining today is more popular than ever, and chefs are creating inventive brines with molasses or beer, while home cooks tend to use buttermilk or sweet tea brines. John T. Edge, writer and director of the Southern Foodways Alliance, gets into the fray in his book *Fried Chicken*, declaring, "By my reckoning, fried chicken must have a bone."

The Chicken Bone Express is the name used to identify the northbound train travels of African Americans during periods of migration out of the South. Fried chicken was the logical food choice for a portable meal for travelers prevented from using whites-only dining establishments. But even before those routes were so-named, in the days just after the Civil War, a group of black women in Gordonsville, Virginia, began to serve food to train travelers who stopped at the prime rail junction of two railroads there. Denied licenses and permits to set up inside the station, they approached the train's opened windows from the track side, offering fried chicken, biscuits, pies, and coffee. Breasts and legs sold for a dime; backs and wings for a nickel. The women called themselves "waiter-carriers" and were welcomed by the travelers as there were no dining cars at that time. Enterprises such as theirs became an important source of income and independence for black women. In honor of those entrepreneurs, a plaque commemorating them was placed near the tracks in front of the Exchange Hotel. Be sure to see the recipe Ode to the Women of Gordonsville, Virginia, on page 58.

Southern cuisine owes a substantial debt to enslaved Africans and African Americans who have contributed their vast knowledge of their own culinary heritage and foodways to the southern table. Many of the most beloved southern foods, such as okra, yams, rice, and so much more, originated in Africa and made their way to our southern farms and kitchens by way of African American cooks who used skills that were passed down orally for generations and then went unacknowledged for generations in writing. Our sideboards would not be what they are today without the tremendous contributions of these unsung cooks.

Today, the South dominates the chart in annual poultry production. The state of Georgia leads the pack, with Alabama, Arkansas, North Carolina, and Mississippi rounding out the top five producers. Georgia produces seven billion pounds of chicken annually—that's about 26 million pounds per day. Americans eat an average of eighty-five to ninety pounds per person annually. And to think it was only about thirty-six pounds per person in 1965.

Gainesville, Georgia, became the "poultry capital of the world" thanks to the work of Jesse Jewell, who was a pioneer in the poultry industry. As the Great Depression drained the feed and seed company his father started, Jewell saw a way to increase the grain sales. He sold grain to cash-poor farmers on credit and gave them baby chicks to raise. When the chicks were grown, Jewell bought the chicks back at a price to provide money to the farmer to pay off the feed debt and to give the farmer a profit from raising the chicks. By 1954 Jewell had his own hatcheries, feed mill, and processing plant, making him the innovator of the first vertically integrated poultry business. He is also credited with introducing frozen chicken to the marketplace. Jewell sold the business in the 1960s, after a very successful career. He was a leader in the industry nationally and lived to see Gainesville grow exponentially in the poultry market, helping to make Georgia the number one producer of chicken in the United States.

With industrialization came low prices, but its cost to chickens was steep. Crowded cages, poor diet, antibiotics, and hormones became the norm. Over time, and with a few well-publicized public health issues arising, consumers began to care about how animals were raised and cared for, as well as the health and safety conditions for poultry workers. The farm-to-table movement introduced small-scale farmers to more and more consumers and has increased the visibility and public awareness of humanely raised and more flavorful meat. Animal welfare laws have been slow to address the plight of the industrial chicken, but that is beginning to change for the better.

The Cultural Chicken

The love we have for chicken in the modern day manifests in many ways, from the popularity of upscale backyard (even urban!) chicken coops, to the ubiquitous store-bought rotisserie chicken, to appreciation for the folk artists who honor the bird in paintings, on furniture, and on textiles. Throughout the United States, a visit to a local artists market, flea market, or decorative arts boutique will confirm how ever-present the chicken is in our lives. Weathervanes with rooster ornaments dating from the eighteenth century to the present are still seen on steeples, as well as adorning both old and new barns alike. (The tradition began when Pope Nicholas I declared late in the ninth century BCE that every church steeple should have a symbolic rooster on top—a symbol of Peter's betrayal of Jesus before the Last Supper.)

In the mid-1800s, a unique "hen fever" swept the country. Special breeding clubs were formed to aid in selective breeding of chickens to produce astonishingly beautiful birds. The Boston Poultry Show of 1849 displayed 1,023 breeds of "rare, curious, and inexpressively beautiful examples of poultry, prized for their beauty, not for their meat." More than 10,000 enthusiasts attended.

In American popular music, chickens strut through song lyrics. Country singer John Anderson sings of getting stuck "behind a chicken truck from Georgia and the feathers were a flyin'" on his way from Alabama to Tennessee on Highway 65. Members of the Zac Brown Band sing of their Georgia roots in their hit "Chicken Fried." And of course the chicken is well represented in children's books and nursery rhymes. Mother Goose gave us The Little Red Hen, Henny-Penny, and Chicken Little.

Even the post office loves chicken. In 1948, the United States Postal Service, in honor of the 100th anniversary of the American poultry industry, issued a commemorative stamp (one of thirty-nine issued that year) featuring a rooster crowing at dawn. Unfortunately, it wasn't a popular stamp. Consumers complained that there were patriotic subjects more deserving of representation on a stamp. It is known by collectors as "the chicken stamp."

For sixty-five years, up until 2014, the Delmava Chicken Festival in Centreville, Maryland, boasted a frying pan ten feet in diameter that fried 800 chicken quarters at a time. Nashville celebrates its signature hot chicken with the Music City Hot Chicken Festival, now in its eighth year. Laurel County, Kentucky, honors Colonel Sanders' first restaurant by celebrating the World Chicken Festival in London, Kentucky. One could devise a wonderful chicken festival tour all around the South and beyond.

Some of you might have heard of the chicken dance—and maybe even performed it with family and friends at a wedding or other celebration. It began as "The Duck Dance," written for the accordion in 1950s Switzerland. By 1970, it became a drinking song at Oktoberfest celebrations. It reached the United States in 1980 when the organizers of the Oktoberfest in Tulsa, Oklahoma, were unable to obtain a duck costume for an appearance on a local TV station. A chicken costume was substituted and the duck dance became the chicken dance.

Peering back in time, we see that the chicken has long been a part of our vernacular language. As far back as ancient Greece, handwriting was compared to chicken scratches. The Dutch later used the word "Henneschrapsel"—hen scratching. In 1579, the English clergyman Stephen Gosson uttered, "I would not have him to count his chickens so soone before they be hatcht," which has origins in the sixth century BCE from Greek storyteller Aesop, whose fables continue to be told today. Slang meanings for chicken abound. We've all heard of "henpecked"—though a term such as "roosterpecked" seems equally justified. "Chicken" can also mean small, as in chicken lobster, or afraid, as in "to chicken out" of doing something. "Running around like a chicken with its head cut off" has special meaning for anyone who has ever cut the head off a chicken. Then there is the game of chicken, the absurd thrill of racing two cars toward each other at high speed, usually on a dark country road. Whoever veers off first to avoid a head-on collision is the loser, though perhaps truly the winner. The phrase "a chicken in every pot" wasn't original to Herbert Hoover's presidential election campaign of 1928, as one might believe. It originated with King Henry IV of France, who said, "If God keeps me, I will make sure that there is no sharecropper in my kingdom who does not have the means to have a chicken in the pot every Sunday!"

Where did these most influential birds come from? It would take volumes to fully illuminate the origins of our favorite culinary bird, but know that the chicken has traipsed nearly every continent. In his book *Why Did the Chicken Cross the World?* Andrew Lawler writes that the chicken was the first avian to spread its wings across the globe as a product of human exploration and travel, meaning the chicken didn't fly—it was carried. It is likely that our modern chickens are descendants of the wild fowl known as red jungle-fowl (*Gallus gallus*), indigenous to India, Malaysia, and China. Carbon-dated ancient bones have revealed that the domesticated bird appeared more than 10,000 years ago in Southeast Asia, and the European world met the domesticated bird in 4000 BCE in Greece. Images of chickens appeared on vases, altars, and tombs in 520 BCE Greece. Egypt embraced the chicken nearly 4,000 years ago when Egyptians invented incubators capable of hatching as many as 10,000 chicks at a time. Page Smith and Charles Daniel tell us in *The Chicken Book* that Roman writers Varro, Plinius, and Columella all wrote about poultry keeping in *De Re Rustica*, a twelve-volume book concerning farming and agriculture, written in the first century CE. Later, the Romans celebrated the culinary bird with a detailed collection of seventeen recipes appearing in *Apicius*, written between 400 and 500 CE. Chickens traveled all across the empire with the Roman army, and it was believed the appetite of the chicken would foretell victory or defeat in battle, with ravenous eating the indication of impending success. When the Romans conquered Britain, they brought chickens with them, although at first the British used the birds for fighting, not for eating. Pacific Islanders, and specifically Polynesians, introduced chickens to South America.

Marcus Empiricus of Bordeaux, a Roman medical writer, wrote in 400–500 BCE that "chicken fat melted and dropped [in the ear] while warm can heal whatsoever disease of the ears." The Renaissance ornithologist Ulisse Aldrovandi wrote in the 1400s, "The genus of chicken offers so great an advantage to men in its use in medicine that there is almost no illness of the body, both internal and external, which does not draw its remedy from these birds. There is no particle of the chicken which does not have its usefulness recognized by the physician." His mother probably already knew that.

The Delicious Chicken

Nearly everyone loves chicken—adults and picky children alike. The meat is so versatile and is equally at home served for a family meal or dressed up for company into something truly special. "Poultry is for the cook what canvas is for a painter," Brillat-Savarin said in *The Physiology of Taste*. New immigrant communities in the South are adding to the culinary conversation. Sandra Gutierrez links Latino cooking with southern cooking in her book *The Southern Latino Table*, while Paul and Angela Knipple, in their book *The World in a Skillet*, demonstrate how immigrant communities have transformed our southern food culture by preparing their native dishes using our regional ingredients. Although we think of fried chicken as southern, immigrants have broadened our tastes with Korean and Latin American flavors, and more.

In fact, the whole world loves chicken. Transcending continents and cultures, it is enjoyed around the world for its affordable, delicious, and nutritious meat. Chicken soup (aka Jewish penicillin) provides comfort (and many people, including me, believe it to be medicinal) to the cold sufferer, no matter the region, and all around the world.

As pork and beef prices continue to rise, poultry prices are expected to remain stable, and worldwide consumption of poultry now surpasses that of pork or beef. Although the industry is lagging in animal rights laws, poultry is much kinder to the environment, with a carbon footprint of half that of pork and a quarter that of beef.

The pleasures of cooking—and eating—a glistening, perfectly roasted whole chicken can't be beat. Obtaining the crispy crust on a piece of fried chicken is achievable. This is where this book comes in. With a few basic rules and a little bit of know-how, you'll soon be serving irresistible chicken dishes, from traditional southern to contemporary and international versions. We'll get started with the basics of acquiring the best chicken, and move right into the techniques.

Chicken Basics

hickens are omnivores—they eat insects, lizards, mice, and nearly anything else that moves. But they can't live on just insects and grass, so on pastured poultry farms, where the flock is truly out of doors and free to roam, they are fed grain as well. Controversy exists over whether what a chicken is fed has an effect on the flavor of the meat. Only in cases where the chicken is fed mixtures containing high amounts of oils will the taste be slightly apparent, and not necessarily in the meat, but in the fat stores of the chicken. So feeding a chicken lemon juice doesn't affect the flavor, but lemon peel, with the essential oils, might influence the taste. But it would be at such a quantity that the bird might not be up to the task.

Heritage breeds are popular on small farms, and many swear by the difference in taste at the table. I do swear by the pastured poultry raised by White Oak Pastures in Bluffton, Georgia, and can taste the difference between it and my grocery store chicken. The chicken is a bit leaner, and the taste is meatier and so much more flavorful.

In chicken nomenclature, roosters are males one year or older, cockerels are males less than one year old, capon is a castrated male, hens are females one year or older, and pullets are females less than one year old.

Buying Chicken

Hands down still the most economical meat protein, chicken is available at prices nearly everyone can afford. Though many shy away from it, learning to cut up a whole chicken not only will save you money; it will also guarantee that the parts all came from one chicken. Purchasing a "whole cut-up" chicken doesn't necessarily mean that all those parts have seen each other before, and rarely are the pairs of cuts (the two thighs, the two breasts, etc.) the same size, which leads to uneven cooking. Undeniably you should purchase the best chicken you can afford. The free-range organic chickens from a local farm will be by far the tastiest you can buy. Look for chickens weighing three to three and a half pounds since they'll be the most flavorful and will cook rather evenly. Avoid the "Sunday roasters," which weigh six or more pounds and are nearly impossible to cook without either drying the breast or undercooking the thighs. Superior taste and texture is found in kosher birds. Not only are these birds processed according to rabbinic law; they are brined to draw out impurities, resulting in a moist and tasty bird. If you're using kosher chicken, skip the brining step in any of the following recipes. I also purchase chicken thighs in large packs since my family is most fond of that cut. I purchase small packages of boneless, skinless chicken breasts for a specific recipe, and I often cut those large breasts into two pieces.

Check to see that the package is very cold in the store and refrigerate it at home as soon as possible. Purchase packages with the farthest sell-by or use-by dates, but no matter the date, refrigerate only one or two days at home, or freeze. Whatever package you purchase, look for those that do not have excess liquid in them, and place the packaged chicken in a disposable plastic bag provided by the store. Keep the package separate from raw fruits and vegetables to avoid any possible cross-contamination. If purchasing a fully cooked rotisserie chicken, purchase a very hot chicken and eat it within two hours, or cut it into pieces and refrigerate. Reheat the chicken thoroughly, to an internal temperature of 165°.

But what package to buy? Poultry labeling is some of the most misunderstood out there. Here is what the labels are supposed to mean, according to the National Chicken Council.

FREE RANGE

There's no precise federal government definition of "free range," so the U.S. Department of Agriculture (USDA) approves these label claims on a case-by-case basis. The USDA generally permits the term to be used if chickens have access to the outdoors for at least some part of the day, whether the chickens choose to go outside or not. But in reality most chickens stay close to water and feed, which is usually located within the chicken house. Chicken labeled as "organic" must also be free-range, but not all free-range chicken is also organic. Less than one percent of chickens nationwide are raised as free range.

FARM-RAISED

All chickens are raised on farms, so any chicken could be labeled "farm-raised," whether it's a picturesque neighboring farm or an immense industrial farm. On restaurant menus it usually refers to chickens raised on a local farm.

NATURAL

Under USDA regulations, a "natural" product has no artificial ingredients, coloring ingredients, or chemical preservatives and is minimally processed, just enough to get it ready to be cooked. Most ready-to-cook chicken can be labeled "natural" if processors choose to do so, but there are no inspections conducted for chicken to earn that label.

ORGANIC

Organic certification for poultry farms, which requires annual in-spections, mandates that access to the outdoors be provided for the chickens but sets no specific standards for the size of the outdoor area, the size of the door between the inside and the outside, or the amount of time the birds spend outdoors. To be labeled USDA Organic, the chicken must be fed a non-GMO vegetarian diet with no toxic synthetic pesticides. Chickens may be fed antibiotics on their first day of life only. Since there are no antibiotics given later, the waste water is not contaminated with them—an important environmental concern. According to the USDA, the organic label does not indicate that the product has safety, quality, or nutritional attributes that are any higher than conventionally raised product. I prefer the taste of organic chicken.

NO HORMONES ADDED

Despite what you may hear, no artificial or added hormones are used in the production of any poultry in the United States. Regu-lations of the Food & Drug Administration prohibit the use of such hormones, so any brand of chicken can be labeled "raised without hormones" or something similar. However, any package of chicken with that type of label must also have a statement that no hormones are used in the production of *any* poultry.

"RAISED WITHOUT ANTIBIOTICS" OR "ANTIBIOTIC-FREE"

"Raised without antibiotics" printed on a package of chicken indicates that the flock was raised without the use of products classified as antibiotics for animal health maintenance, disease prevention, or treatment of disease. Animal health products not classified as antibiotics (such as some coccidiostats, which control protozoal parasites) may still be used. The designation "antibiotic-free" is not allowed to be used directly on a packaging label but may be found in marketing materials not regulated by the USDA. It means the same thing as "raised without antibiotics." All chicken is antibiotic-free in the sense that no antibiotic residues are present in the meat, kidneys, or liver due to the regulated withdrawal period. The withdrawal period can be as short as twenty-four hours or as long as five days, depending on how long it takes for the residue of a certain antibiotic to fall below allowable levels. Antibiotics therefore are not present in the poultry we eat, but any antibiotics used before the withdrawal period are an environmental concern, particularly for waste water.

ENHANCED CHICKEN PRODUCTS

Some fresh (raw and uncooked) chicken products are "enhanced" with chicken broth or a similar solution. The presence and percentage of the broth or other solution must be stated clearly and the actual ingredients listed on the label. Both enhanced and non-enhanced products are currently available in the marketplace. Sodium is used in the broth or solution of some enhanced products, and is noted on the label.

"RETAINED WATER"

A "retained water" statement, such as "May contain up to 6% retained water" or "Less than 4% retained water," is often found on packages of fresh poultry. The USDA prohibits retention of moisture in meat and poultry except for the amount that results from essential safety procedures, such as chilling processed chickens in ice-cold water to reduce their temperature and retard the growth of spoilage bacteria and other microorganisms. If any moisture is retained by the product after this procedure, it must be stated on the label.

ALL-VEGETABLE DIET

Poultry feed is made primarily from corn and soybean meal. Poultry feed sometimes includes some processed protein and fats and oils from meat and poultry by-products. The composition of all animal feed ingredients used in the United States is regulated by the Association of American Feed Control Officials (AAFCO). If the chicken company chooses not to use these ingredients, the feed would contain no ingredients derived from animals and could be described as "all vegetable."

MADE IN THE USA

Nearly all the chickens and chicken products sold in the United States come from chickens hatched, raised, and processed in the United States. The only exception is a small amount imported from Canada, which has food safety and quality standards equal to our own.

AIR-CHILLED POULTRY

"Air-chilled" is a new term to appear on packages of processed chicken. After chickens are slaughtered, they are plunged into hot-water tanks to remove the feathers. Conventional processors then plunge the birds into ice-cold baths, where the birds can take on water. It is also one of the steps in processing during which salmonella can be spread. Some facilities are now using air-chilled chambers, essentially refrigerators instead of water baths, which cool the birds quickly and bypass the potential for water retention and lessen salmonella exposure.

Handling Raw Chicken

I keep a package of inexpensive disposable plastic gloves in my kitchen. Although they are handy for so many kitchen duties, I primarily use them for handling raw chicken. Wash hands thoroughly with hot soapy water before and after handling poultry.

Storing Chicken

Chicken spoils quickly in the refrigerator. Usually if there is an odor before or after opening the package, the chicken should be thrown away. If you are not cooking your chicken within two days, it needs to be packaged for the freezer.

If you're freezing it for a short time, up to two weeks, chicken may be frozen unopened, in its original packaging. For long storage, open the package and wrap the chicken tightly in plastic wrap or foil, and then place it in a resealable plastic bag, removing as much air as possible. It isn't the freezing that degrades the meat, it is the air the meat is exposed to that leads to freezer burn. For chicken breasts (or any cuts that might be used singly), wrap them individually, then move them to a large plastic bag. I keep chicken backs and wing tips in a resealable plastic freezer bag, and when I have enough, I'll make stock (page 136) and freeze it in one- or two-cup portions. If you're freezing stock in plastic freezer bags, place them flat on a baking sheet until frozen, then stack as necessary. In all cases, take the time to mark the date and the contents. Everything tends to look the same once it's frozen.

Thawing Frozen Chicken

Thawing should be done in the refrigerator. A three-pound whole chicken will take twenty-four hours to thaw. Tempting though it is, avoid thawing meat on the kitchen counter. If you are in a hurry, frozen chicken may be thawed still wrapped in its airtight packaging submerged in a large pot of cold water. Change the water every thirty minutes.

Let's Begin

Rinsing chicken is a thing of the past. Although it's a hard habit for some to break, experts agree that rinsing a chicken allows potentially harmful bacteria to spread around the sink and counter. Skip the rinse and pat the chicken dry with paper towels and discard the towels. I keep my sink full of hot soapy water while I'm working with chicken so I have a place ready to dump my dirty knife, scissors, cutting board, and anything else exposed to raw chicken. You will want to rinse a chicken after it has been brined, however, to remove any excess salted water. Place the chicken in a colander in the sink and run it under cold water. Patting the chicken dry increases the chance of having crispy skin, and prepares the skin for a brush of butter or oil, or a soak in a bath of marinade.

When you're ready to begin cooking a whole chicken, remove any packets or parts from the cavity and discard (unless you're saving the liver for a cook's treat, or the neck for stock). Many whole birds sold today do not have anything in the cavity. Whether whole or parts, the next step is to trim any excess fat and skin from the chicken. Whole chickens usually have excess skin and fat around the opening to the cavity. Frequently chicken thighs will have extra skin that is large enough to encase the whole thigh. Trim the excess and discard. When you're preparing wings, remove the tip end of the wing and save for stock or discard. Some recipes call for disjointing the wing, which is easily done with a knife by slicing through the joint separating what now is called a drum or drumette and a flat.

People often overcook boneless, skinless chicken breasts, and it's almost always because the breast is very thick in the middle or on one end and thin on the sides. Flatten chicken breasts between two sheets of wax paper with a meat pounder, mallet, or rolling pin to achieve an even thickness. This will reduce the overall cooking time and yield moister meat. Chicken breasts are ghastly large these days, so I frequently cut them in half, at least, for individual servings. In my recipes here, a boneless, skinless chicken breast is about five ounces of meat. When a recipe calls for four chicken breasts, assess the size available to determine if you should purchase just two and cut them in half.

Cutting Up a Whole Chicken

Fit a rimmed baking sheet with a cutting board. Pat the chicken dry and place it breast-side-up onto the board. Using a sharp knife, cut through the joint where the leg connects to the body of the chicken. If you have trouble finding it, slice through the skin at that joint, then feel from underneath the "hip" joint and push up while pushing the "knee" of the leg down. Repeat for the other leg. Similarly, cut through the joint of the leg at the top of the drumstick, separating the thigh and the drumstick. Turn the chicken breast-side-down. In a similar fashion, cut each wing away from the body by bending it out and down and cutting through the joint. Remove the tips of the wings and reserve for stock or discard. Cut through the joint of the wing, separating it into the drum and the flat. Cut through the chicken on either side of the backbone to remove it. I prefer kitchen shears to cut out the back. Reserve for stock. Left now with just the breast, slice through the cartilage to separate the breasts into two halves. Usually the breasts are very large, so cut each breast in half widthwise.

Seasoning Raw Chicken

To avoid contaminating the salt shaker and pepper mill with chicken juices from your hands, mix the salt and pepper needed for the recipe in a small ramekin. Discard any remaining in the ramekin after cooking begins.

Techniques

ROASTING

The gold standard for a tender, glistening bird is our classic Sunday roast chicken. Sliding fat under the skin keeps the breast moist, and brushing the skin with butter or oil seals the skin and helps to create the crispy delight we all love to sneak a pinch of. Although some disagree, I find that roasting a whole chicken on a rack and turning it from side to side, then on its back, will produce a very fine bird with moist and tender fully cooked meat and crispy skin. While it may be daunting the first time you turn the chicken, it will come easier the second time, especially as you refine which tools in your kitchen serve the purpose best. I use a long wooden spoon and a long pair of spring-loaded tongs.

BROILING AND GRILLING

Broiling is a direct-heat method requiring the chicken to be protected by a marinade or a good brush of oil. It must be watched to prevent overcooking. When grilling, prepare both a direct heat and indirect heat section. Start the chicken (also marinated or brushed) over the direct heat on the grill, then move the chicken away from direct heat to fully cook.

POACHING

For delicate, moist chicken to be used in chicken salad or other cooked chicken recipes, poaching is the best method. Select a pot with a lid that will hold the chicken with not a lot of extra room (makes for more flavorful broth in the end). Cover the chicken with cold water and cook over medium heat until the water reaches about 190–200°. Cover the pan with the lid and remove it from the heat. Let stand for 45 minutes for a whole chicken, down to about 15 minutes for boneless, skinless chicken breasts. Cool and use as needed. The resting period off the heat allows the chicken to become fully cooked and is very gentle on the meat, preventing the chicken from getting tough and stringy, which happens when the meat is violently boiled.

BRAISING

Braising is a classic technique where the chicken is browned and then partially submerged in liquid. The browning adds flavor to the dish, and the liquid tenderizes the chicken. The collagen and fat from the meat help thicken the liquid and turn it into a great sauce. The pan and the fat must be hot before adding the chicken, skin-side-down, for the optimal deep golden brown color we love. Avoid moving the chicken once you've added it to the fat, otherwise it will stick. The skin releases from the pan once it's browned. I love braising chicken, and its when this technique is called for that you'll see the most variety in the recipes in this book as nearly any liquid may be used, from water to stock to wine, and can include most any herbs and seasonings. It's a creative cook's dream.

STEWING

Stewing a chicken is similar to poaching, but stewing involves a much longer cooking time. If an old rooster had outlived his usefulness, he would be stewed since the meat would be tough and require long, slow simmering to tenderize.

SAUTÉING

When sautéing chicken, only a small amount of oil is used to seal in the juices, and the chicken is turned frequently during cooking. The primary difference in sautéing and frying is in the amount of oil used.

FRYING

Frying creates the crust we love on chicken. Most frequently, the chicken is coated in flour and cooked in hot oil to seal in all the rich, juicy flavor of the chicken. Covering the surrounding area adjacent to the frying pan with aluminum foil makes for easy clean up.

Equipment

A large heavy skillet is essential for most chicken recipes, whether cast iron or stainless steel. I don't achieve the same browning results in a nonstick pan, but as those materials continue to evolve, some are sufficient for browning. For frying, I prefer my Dutch oven, which is tall enough to reduce spatters. For pounding chicken breasts flat, I use a meat mallet, but any meat pounder will do, and even a rolling pin can suffice. When flouring chicken, and holding chicken between batches, it's helpful to have wire racks that fit into your rimmed baking sheets. There is quite a bit of "scraping the brown bits" off the bottom of a skillet or Dutch oven in these recipes as so many of them called for browning the chicken pieces. A flat wooden spatula is the best tool for the job, and it spares those surfaces from being scarred from a metal spatula. Spring-loaded tongs have long tips that can gently turn the chicken in the pan, whereas old-fashioned tongs might disturb the browned crust. Avoid using a fork as piercing the meat lets the juices run out. Using a good-quality instant-read thermometer is essential to confirm the chicken is cooked through.

Tests for Doneness

Old recipes have many tips on testing the doneness of chicken, from wiggling the legs to piercing the thigh looking for clear juices, but there is only one way to truly know your chicken is properly cooked. Chicken breasts must reach 160–165° and chicken thighs 170–175° on an instant-read thermometer inserted into the thickest portions to verify doneness.

The Cooking

The mouth-watering recipes for whole chicken, whole cut-up chicken, and chicken thighs, breasts, and wings that follow offer something for everyone. Whether you use an oven, stovetop, or grill—there's a recipe here for every mode and every season. I hope you'll find a favorite here to share at your family table.

The Whole Bird

Nothing says Sunday dinner like a beautifully roasted whole chicken, moist and tender, with glistening, crispy skin adorning the family table. To make any bird your most-requested recipe, follow the simple steps here for a tender bird every time. Brining is a time-tested path to moist poultry. But you'll also want to try the other cooking methods featured here, such as using a clay pot, rotisserie, or even a Bundt pan for juicy chicken. Simple seasoning lets the true flavor shine through, but experiment to make these recipes your own. Your bird will make a grand centerpiece using any of the various methods offered here.

For recipes that call for cut-up chicken, I encourage you to cut it up yourself. It's easy to do once you've done it a couple of times, and you'll be rewarded with evenly cooked meat. Remember that the parts in a store-packaged whole chicken have never met each other before and are likely to vary greatly in size.

Perfect Roast Chicken

A sign of a great cook is his or her ability to roast a chicken. It seems so easy—just pop the bird in a pan and stick it in the oven, but just taking a few steps in between will produce a moist and tender bird, fit for a Sunday mealtime centerpiece. And if you really want to make life easy this week, roast two birds at the same time, carving the second one for use later in the week.

Brining is a cook's insurance that the bird will be moist, and sealing the skin by coating it in butter before roasting results in the golden, crispy skin we love. Sliding butter under the skin keeps the breast tender and flavorful. Turning the bird during roasting helps keep the breast from drying out before the legs and thighs are fully cooked.

Consider mixing herbs and spices into the softened butter before placing it under the skin. The fat transfers the flavors into the breast meat more intensely than when the flavorings are added to the brine. Use one teaspoon finely chopped herbs per tablespoon of butter. Try thyme, rosemary, parsley, garlic, curry or chili powder, or minced ginger.

½ cup salt
½ cup granulated sugar
1 (3½-pound) whole chicken
Canola oil or cooking spray
3 tablespoons butter, softened, divided
Freshly ground black pepper
1 lemon
1–2 sprigs fresh rosemary

Dissolve the salt and sugar in 2 quarts of water in a pot or tub large enough to submerge the whole chicken under the water. Add the chicken and refrigerate for 1–4 hours. When ready to cook, preheat the oven to 400°. Place an oiled (or sprayed) v-shaped rack in a large roasting pan. Remove the bird from the brine to a colander placed in the sink, rinse under cold water, pat dry, and move to a cutting board. Using your fingers, carefully loosen the skin from the breast meat. Spoon 1 tablespoon of the soften butter under the skin of one side of the breast. Spread the butter over the breast by massaging it through the skin. Repeat with the other side of the breast. Rub the skin of the entire bird with the remaining butter and season with pepper. Cut both ends off the lemon and then cut the lemon in half horizontally. Insert the lemon halves and rosemary in the cavity of the chicken.

Move the chicken to the oiled rack, placing it on its side (one wing facing up). Let it rest at room temperature for 30 minutes. Roast for 15 minutes. Using long tongs or wadded paper towels, rotate the chicken in the rack to the other side so that the other wing is facing up. Roast for 15 minutes. Rotate the chicken again so that the breast is now facing up and continue roasting for 20–25 minutes, or until the thickest part of the thigh reaches 175° on an instant-read thermometer. Remove the chicken to a cutting board and allow it to rest for 10–15 minutes, then carve and serve.

BRINING

Soaking a chicken in a solution of water and salt before roasting adds moisture to the meat, resulting in a very succulent, juicy chicken. The salt denatures the proteins in the muscle fibers—actually unwinding the protein bundles in the muscle—thereby tenderizing the meat and allowing the fibers to absorb the flavor of the brine. To make the brine, in a pot or tub large enough to submerge the whole chicken under the water, dissolve ½ cup kosher salt and ½ cup granulated sugar (optional) in 2 quarts of water. Add the chicken and refrigerator for 1–4 hours. If you are brining only wings and/or drumsticks, brine for only 30 minutes. Aromatics such as bay leaves, thyme, or rosemary may be added to the brining liquid, if desired. Always discard the brine after use.

Clay Pot Whole Chicken

Romertopf brought the clay baker to the American kitchen in 1967. It remained a kitchen staple through the 1970s but then faded in popularity. If you happen to have one in your cupboard or storage area, bring it out to roast a truly moist whole chicken. As with slow cookers, the clay baker does not produce perfectly browned crispy skin. To remedy that, before roasting, you can brown the outside of the chicken in an oiled skillet over medium-high heat, turning frequently until the skin is lightly browned. I think it's tedious to brown the chicken on the stove, so I use my clay pot when I want to have extra-moist chicken around for use in dishes calling for precooked chicken such as chicken pot pie, chicken salad, and the like. This way I don't have to worry about whether the chicken is browning too fast. Submerge both the top and the bottom of the baker in cold water for 15–20 minutes before using, or according to the manufacturer's instructions.

MAKES 4–6 SERVINGS

1 clay pot baker, soaked in water
1 (3½-pound) chicken
2 tablespoons butter, softened
Salt
Freshly ground black pepper

Pat the chicken dry and move it to the bottom of the prepared clay baker. Rub the butter over the entire chicken. Sprinkle evenly with salt and pepper. Let it rest at room temperature for 30 minutes. Cover with the lid and place it in a cold oven. Set the oven temperature to 400° and roast the chicken until the thickest part of the thigh reaches 175° on an instant-read thermometer, about 1 hour and 15 minutes.

Transfer the clay baker to a folded kitchen towel or hot pads. (The baker cracks easily when in contact with a contrasting temperature.) Remove the chicken to a cutting board and let it rest for 10–15 minutes before carving. Often the bird barely holds together enough for traditional carving, and I just gently release the parts with a knife and large spoon, and transfer to plates.

VARIATION ❀ CLAY POT WHOLE CHICKEN WITH VEGETABLES
Place ½ pound small new potatoes and wedges of one small onion in the bottom of the clay baker. Sprinkle ½ cup white wine or chicken broth over the potatoes and onions. Add the chicken and follow the baking instructions as above.

Straight Up Bundt Pan
Roast Chicken

If you are a lover of crisp roast chicken skin, grab your Bundt pan. Roasting a chicken vertically exposes a larger surface area of the chicken to the heat and produces the kind of skin the cook secretly wants to pinch off before the bird ever reaches the dining table. Many household cabinets harbor a small piece of wire sculpture in its dark recesses called a vertical roaster. If you don't have this hidden jewel, and you haven't been to a yard sale recently, the Bundt pan performs the same function, and I think it's even easier to use.

Occasionally I'll toss a few cut up potatoes or carrots in the bottom of the pan before adding the chicken. Any variety of root vegetable would be welcome. No need to alter the cooking time, so long as the vegetables are cut in 1-inch (or smaller) pieces.

MAKES 4–6 SERVINGS

---

1 (3½-pound) chicken
1 lemon, quartered
1 medium onion, cut into 8 wedges
6 sprigs fresh thyme
1 tablespoon olive oil or butter
Salt
Freshly ground black pepper

Preheat the oven to 425°. Pat the chicken dry with paper towels. Arrange the lemon, onion, and thyme (and any vegetables you might be using) evenly around the bottom of a Bundt pan. Rub the chicken with the oil or butter and season with salt and pepper. Crimp a small piece of aluminum foil over the open center hole of the pan. Mount the chicken on the pan with the wings up. Move the Bundt pan to a rimmed baking sheet. Bake the chicken for 60 minutes, or until the thickest part of the thigh registers 175° on an instant-read thermometer. Remove the chicken to a platter and let it rest for 10 minutes before carving. Strain the juices from the bottom of the Bundt pan into a small saucepan, simmer until slightly reduced, and serve with the chicken.

Weeknight Roast Chicken

To speed up the roasting time for a whole bird, "spatchcock" the chicken by removing the backbone and flattening out the chicken. Heavy-duty kitchen scissors or poultry shears make easy work of cutting out the backbone. Roasting the chicken at a high temperature also speeds up the process. If I use this recipe on a weeknight, I usually don't brine the chicken first, but you may if time is not of the essence (page 27).

MAKES 4–6 SERVINGS

1 (3½-pound) chicken
5 tablespoons butter, softened, divided
Salt
Freshly ground black pepper

Pat the chicken dry and place it breast-side-down on a cutting board. Remove the backbone by cutting along both sides of the bone. Discard the bone (or freeze for making stock, page 136). Turn the chicken skin-side-up and open the chicken to lay it flat, pressing down with the heel of your hand on the breastbone until it "cracks," leaving a flattened bird.

Using your fingers, carefully loosen the skin from the breast meat. Spoon 1 tablespoon of the butter under the skin of one side of the breast. Spread the butter over the breast by massaging it through the skin. Repeat with other side of the breast. Rub the skin of the entire bird with the remaining butter and season with salt and pepper.

Move the chicken to a shallow roasting pan lined with a flat rack, skin-side-up. Let it rest at room temperature for 30 minutes. Preheat the oven to 450°. Roast the chicken 45 minutes, or until the thickest part of the thigh reaches 175° on an instant-read thermometer. Remove the chicken to a cutting board and allow it to rest for 10–15 minutes before carving.

VARIATION ✳ EXTRA CRISPY WEEKNIGHT ROAST CHICKEN
Before rubbing the chicken with butter, return it to the refrigerator, uncovered, for several hours or overnight. This dries out the skin, aiding in browning and crisping. Rub with butter before baking.

Port Wine–Glazed Chicken and Figs

Preserves, jams, and jellies are handy ingredients for creating easy glazes and sauces for poultry and meats. The port tints the skin, yielding a darker, richer color and adds a deep, full flavor. I fall in love with figs each year as if it is the first time I've ever tasted them. If fresh are unavailable, halve dried figs, add them to the sauce, and pour the sauce around the chicken before it goes in the oven to bake.

MAKES 4 SERVINGS

1 (3½-pound) chicken
Salt
Freshly ground black pepper
3–4 sprigs fresh rosemary
½ cup fig preserves
¼ cup ruby port
12 fresh figs, stemmed and halved
Wild rice, for serving

Preheat the oven to 375°. Pat the chicken dry and sprinkle it liberally with salt and pepper. Insert the rosemary into the cavity. Transfer the bird to a small baking dish. Stir together the fig preserves and port in a small bowl. Baste the chicken with the fig sauce and move the chicken to the oven, reserving the sauce. Cook about 1 hour, basting two to three times with the pan drippings during cooking. After 30 minutes of baking time, toss the fresh figs in with the reserved sauce and pour this over and around chicken. Continue cooking until the thickest part of the thigh registers 175° on an instant-read thermometer. Remove the chicken to a cutting board and let it rest for 10 minutes before carving. Serve with wild rice, if desired.

Frances Graubart's
1940s Rotisserie Chicken

My husband came to our marriage with a large countertop electric oven complete with a rotisserie. At first glance, all I saw was a gigantic space hog. Countertop? I don't think so. We let it languish in our basement for several years, until one day my husband craved the taste of his mother Francis Graubart's rotisserie chicken she used to make when he was growing up. Up from the basement it came, after we cleared a wide berth for its temporary home. After giving the oven a good cleaning, my husband deftly assembled the rotisserie and prepared the bird simply with salt, pepper, and garlic powder. We set the oven temperature and turned on the motor. About ninety minutes later we enjoyed the best chicken dinner we had ever cooked. Although the rotisserie still didn't earn a permanent space on the kitchen counter, it is kept handy on a shelf in the garage, just outside the kitchen door. Your regular oven may have a rotisserie assembly, or you may have one for your grill. Either way, the bird bastes in its own juices, keeping the entire bird moist and tender.

MAKES 4–6 SERVINGS

1 (3½-pound) chicken
Salt
Freshly ground black pepper
2 teaspoons garlic powder

Pat the chicken dry and season evenly with salt and pepper and the garlic powder. Let the chicken rest for 30 minutes at room temperature. Secure the chicken to the rotisserie assembly and roast for 1 hour at 350°. Check the temperature of the meat and continue to roast until the thickest part of the thigh reaches 175° on an instant-read thermometer. Remove the chicken from the rotisserie and let it rest on a cutting board for 10–15 minutes before carving.

Herbed Chicken Under a Brick

A spatchcocked, flattened chicken is moist and flavorful, and marinating this chicken in a Tuscan-style marinade for four to six hours will result in tasty, crusty skin. If bricks are not available, use a heavy, slightly smaller skillet over a sheet of aluminum foil to place on top of the chicken.

After testing various methods, I've determined that finishing the chicken in the oven results in a moister bird.

MAKES 4 SERVINGS

1 (3½-pound) chicken
¼ cup olive oil
2 tablespoons chopped fresh rosemary
2 tablespoons chopped fresh thyme
½ teaspoon salt
½ teaspoon freshly ground black pepper
4 garlic cloves, chopped
½ cup fresh lemon juice
Two foil-covered bricks

Pat the chicken dry and place it breast-side-down on a cutting board. Remove the backbone by cutting along both sides of the bone. Discard the bone (or freeze it for making stock, page 136). Turn the chicken over and press down with the heel of your hand on the breastbone until it "cracks," leaving a flattened bird. Move the chicken to a large resealable plastic bag. Whisk together the olive oil, herbs, salt, pepper, garlic, and lemon juice in a small bowl. Pour the mixture over the chicken, turn to coat, and refrigerate for 4–6 hours.

When ready to cook, preheat the oven to 400°. Heat a large oven-proof skillet over medium-high heat. Move the chicken, skin-side-down, to the skillet. Discard the marinade. Place the bricks on the chicken to keep it flat. Cook for 10–15 minutes, or until the skin is nicely browned and crispy. Remove the bricks and turn the chicken skin-side-up and transfer the chicken to the hot oven. Cook for 15–20 minutes, or until the thickest part of the thigh reaches 175° on an instant-read thermometer. Remove the chicken to a cutting board and let it rest for 10 minutes before carving.

VARIATION ❋ GRILLED CHICKEN UNDER A BRICK Prepare the grill to medium-high heat on one half of the grill and low heat on the other half. Place the chicken skin-side-down over the hotter side and place bricks on top of the chicken. Cook for 6–7 minutes, remove the bricks, and flip the chicken over to cook the other side for 3–4 minutes. Move the chicken to the cooler half of the grill and continue cooking until the thickest part of the thigh reaches 175° on an instant-read thermometer.

Smothered Chicken

Smothered Chicken is a classic southern comfort food dish. Weighing down the chicken while cooking has been traditional. Mississippi native Craig Claiborne, the famous New York Times *food writer, said that's where the name came in — the chicken was smothered with a weighted skillet or bricks. I always thought the delicious gravy that smothered the chicken was how it got its name. No matter what you call it, it's fabulous.*

MAKES 4–6 SERVINGS

1 (3½-pound) chicken
Salt
Freshly ground black pepper
2 tablespoons unsalted butter, divided
2 medium onions, sliced
Two foil-covered bricks
2 tablespoons all-purpose flour
1½ cups chicken stock or broth

Pat the chicken dry and place it breast-side-down on a cutting board. Remove the backbone by cutting along both sides of the bone. Discard the bone (or freeze it for making stock, page 136). Turn the chicken over and press down with the heel of your hand on the breastbone until it "cracks," leaving a flattened bird. Season with salt and pepper.

When ready to cook, preheat the oven to 400°. Heat a large oven-proof skillet over medium-high heat. Add 2 tablespoons of the butter and sauté the onions for 10–15 minutes, or until browned. Remove the onions and set aside. Add the remaining butter to the hot skillet and move the chicken, skin-side-down, to the skillet. Place the bricks on the chicken to keep it flat. Cook for 10–15 minutes, or until the skin is nicely browned and crispy. Remove the bricks and turn the chicken skin-side-up; cover with bricks and cook for 15 minutes. Remove the chicken to a plate and pour off all but 2 tablespoons of the fat from the pan. Reduce the heat to medium and whisk in the flour, stirring constantly, until the flour is incorporated and turns a medium brown. Gradually pour in the stock or broth and stir until slightly thickened. Return the onions to the pan, stir, and add the chicken. Continue cooking the chicken for 15–20 minutes, or until the thickest part of the thigh reaches 175° on an instant-read thermometer. Remove the chicken to a cutting board and let it rest for 10 minutes before carving into serving pieces. Coat each piece with some the sauce and pass the rest at the table.

Carolina Chicken Bog

Both North and South Carolina lay claim to this soul-warming dish, and its name evokes the bogginess of the swamps of the low country, as well as to the appearance of the chicken in the dish—bogged down by the rice and broth. I learned from Nancie McDermott, author of Southern Soups and Stews, *that a "bog-off" takes place annually in Loris, South Carolina, where bogs are made outdoors in gigantic cast-iron caldrons every October. Many Asian cultures have a similar dish in which rice is cooked in stock as a breakfast meal, with various meats or fish optional, or as a meal for those recovering from illness. Here the chicken is simmered gently and removed from the bone, and the bones are then cooked as for stock, and strained. The chicken meat is returned to the pot with the stock and seasoned with onion and sausage. The rice is added at the end and emerges as slick, individual grains, surrounded by the chicken and broth. Individual bowls are topped with sliced fresh green onions and parsley.*

Carolina Gold is a Revolutionary War–era grain returning to popularity from heirloom seeds. Known as a "new crop rice," it's milled and shipped without the heat-drying process used in commercial rice harvesting. The rice still has a hint of the aroma of the fields. Any long-grain rice may be substituted.

If you are even slightly under the weather, a bowl of this nourishing bog will set you straight.

MAKES 6 SERVINGS

---

1 (3½-pound) chicken
1 medium onion, quartered
1–2 carrots, sliced ¼ inch thick
1 celery rib, sliced ¼ inch thick, with no leaves
1 bay leaf
12 black peppercorns
4–6 sprigs thyme (optional)
8 parsley stems (optional)
2 garlic cloves, unpeeled (optional)

8 cups chicken stock or broth
8 ounces andouille sausage or kielbasa, sliced $\frac{1}{2}$ inch thick
1 cup rice, Carolina Gold preferred
1 teaspoon freshly ground black pepper
Salt (optional)
2 tablespoons butter
2 green onions, sliced (optional)
3 tablespoons chopped fresh parsley (optional)

Place the chicken, onion, carrots, celery, bay leaf, and pepper-corns (and the thyme, parsley stems, and garlic, if using) in a large stockpot. Pour in the chicken stock or broth. (It's not necessary for the breast to be completely submerged.) Bring to a simmer over medium heat, then reduce the heat to low. Cover and simmer for 1 hour. Remove from the heat and let sit, covered, for 1 hour.

Remove the chicken to a foil-lined rimmed baking sheet to cool. When cool enough to handle, remove the meat from the bones to a bowl, shredding the larger pieces. Discard the skin. Return the bones to the pot of stock, and refrigerate the chicken until needed. Bring the stock with the bones to a simmer and cook until the liquid is reduced to about 6 cups. Strain through cheesecloth or a fine-mesh sieve. Discard the solids. Either refrigerate overnight (to remove the chilled fat) or defat using a gravy separator.

To finish the bog, stir the chicken and sausage into the de-fatted stock. Bring to a simmer over medium heat. Once sim-mering, taste to determine seasoning. Reduce the heat to low and stir in the rice and pepper and season with salt, if needed. Cook for about 25 minutes, stirring occasionally, until the rice is cooked and the dish is stew-like. Stir in the butter and ladle the stew into bowls. Sprinkle each serving with green onion and parsley, if desired. Serve hot.

Chicken Mull

I entered a fascinating discussion on social media about the history of chicken mull with Michael Phillips, whose family has lived in the Commerce, Georgia, area since 1784. Chicken mull has been popular dish there dating back to perhaps as early as the late 1890s, when saltine crackers were widely available in the south. A restaurant in Nicholson, Georgia, located between Athens and Commerce puts out a big sign on the highway when it has this very filling, easy-to-make, cold-weather dish on the menu. Michael suggests this dish was very popular during the Depression era, but it remains a favorite since it serves a crowd inexpensively. Many volunteer fire departments in the rural areas of Jackson, Banks, and Madison Counties have chicken mull fund-raisers. Every fall from the early 1960s into the 1980s, during the height of the University of Georgia football season, Michael's father, Aubry Phillips, would throw a big party where he'd cook chicken mull in giant cast-iron pots in their backyard, and hundreds would attend, including the entire police and sheriff's departments, along with the mayor and all the city councilmen and county commissioners, and his loyal customers from his two car dealerships in Athens. Bear Creek, North Carolina, where residents claim chicken mull was invented, hosts an annual Chicken Mull Festival. But they use vegetables in their recipe, and Michael tells me no self-respecting Northeast Georgia cook would ever put vegetables in chicken mull.

Michael doesn't want to claim the following as THE *chicken mull recipe because, if he did, he says, half the church ladies in Commerce would be after him with an iron skillet.*

1 large chicken (about 4½ to 5 pounds)
2 cups chicken stock or broth
4 tablespoons unsalted butter
3 cups whole milk
3–4 sleeves Saltine crackers, plus more for serving
Salt
Freshly ground black pepper
Hot sauce, for serving

Place the chicken in a large stockpot with enough water to cover the chicken and bring it to a boil over high heat. Reduce the heat and simmer the chicken for 2–3 hours. Remove the chicken from the pot and remove the meat from the bones; chop or shred the meat and discard the bones. Strain the cooking water into a fresh pot set over medium heat. Add the cooked chicken and chicken stock or broth. Stir in the butter and milk. As the soup heats, crush and stir in a sleeve of crackers. Add additional sleeves until the mixture resembles oatmeal. Season to taste with salt and pepper. Pass the hot sauce at the table along with additional crackers.

Chicken with Forty Cloves of Garlic

James Beard, America's beloved cookbook author and teacher, introduced this Provençal dish to the American palate. Until the recipe was well-circulated, diners doubted that something with that much garlic could even be edible. Edible it is, and the roasted garlic cloves are a culinary treat. There are numerous methods for removing the skin from the cloves. I put the heads of garlic in a bowl and place another bowl of the same size inverted over the first bowl to form a sphere (this can also be done with any two containers that match in size). Shake the bowl vigorously for 10–20 seconds. The paper skins will fall off.

Serve this dish with good bread upon which you should spread the miraculous melting garlic cloves. Ina Garten and Martha Stewart both use fresh thyme in their versions, and James Beard uses tarragon in his. For this classic dish, the choice is yours.

MAKES 4–6 SERVINGS

1 (3½-pound) chicken, cut into 8 pieces
2 tablespoons canola oil
3 heads garlic, peeled
½ cup dry vermouth
¾ cup chicken stock or broth
6–8 sprigs fresh thyme (optional)
2 tablespoons chopped fresh tarragon (optional)

Preheat the oven to 350°.

Pat the chicken dry. Heat the oil over medium-high heat in a large Dutch oven. Cook the chicken, skin-side-down, in batches if necessary to avoid overcrowding, until the skin is nicely browned, about 5 or so minutes. Turn the pieces over to brown the other side for 3–4 minutes. (If you're cooking in batches, remove the chicken as it is browned to a platter. Repeat with remaining chicken pieces and return the chicken to the pan.) Scatter the garlic in the pot and add the vermouth and stock or broth. Scrape the bottom of the pot to loosen any browned bits. Add the thyme, if using, or sprinkle the chicken with the tarragon, if using. Cover with a lid and bake for 30 minutes. Remove the lid and continue baking for about 20 minutes, or until the chicken is cooked through and the thickest part of the thigh reaches 175° on an instant-read thermometer. Remove the chicken from the oven and let it rest for 5–10 minutes before serving.

Country Captain

In Mastering the Art of Southern Cooking, *Nathalie Dupree and I conquered the mystery of the origins of Country Captain, a popular dish of cut-up chicken in a tomato-curry sauce. Curries were popular in the South in the 1800s due to the rigorous spice trade into the ports of Charleston and Savannah, but the recipes rarely included tomatoes until much later. The dish gained national fame after it became a favorite of Franklin Delano Roosevelt. It was served to him in Warm Springs, Georgia, at the home of Mrs. Bullard.* She had taken the recipe from The International Cookbook: Over 3,300 Recipes Gathered from All over the World, Including Many Never Before Published in English, *a two-volume set written by the former chef of Delmonico's, Alessandro Filippini, and published in 1914. Mrs. Bullard selected the recipe and gave it to her cook, Arie Mullins, who served it to Roosevelt, who loved it. Later on, Roosevelt's favorite cook, Daisy Bonner, prepared the dish to be served to the patients at the polio treatment facility in Warm Springs, which Roosevelt frequented. There are variations galore, some with coconut, others with bacon, thyme, or parsley (as in Filippini's version). Some deep fry the chicken for this recipe, and still others serve it in the tradition of a curry, with chutney. Nathalie Dupree removes the chicken from the bones and returns the meat to the skillet for the final cooking, thus making it a fork-friendly meal. The recipe makes a gracious plenty, so don't hesitate to freeze portions for another meal if you aren't serving a crowd.*

2 whole chickens (3½–4 pounds each), cut into 8 pieces each
4 tablespoons butter
1 tablespoon canola or olive oil
1–2 medium onions, chopped
2 red bell peppers, cored, seeded, and chopped
4 garlic cloves, finely chopped
1/4–1/2 teaspoon cayenne pepper
2–3 teaspoons curry powder
2 (28-ounce) cans Italian plum tomatoes, liquid reserved
Salt
Freshly ground black pepper
1 cup currants or raisins
Shredded coconut (optional)
6 slices bacon, cooked crisp (optional)
1 teaspoon dried thyme (optional)
½ cup chopped fresh parsley (optional)
8 cups cooked rice, for serving
1 cup blanched, toasted sliced almonds, for garnish
Chutney (optional)

Pat the chicken dry. Heat the butter and oil over medium heat in a large heavy skillet and, in batches if necessary to avoid overcrowding the skillet, add the chicken, skin-side-down, cooking until nicely browned, about 5 or so minutes. Turn the chicken pieces over with tongs, and brown for 2–3 minutes on the second side. Remove the chicken as it is browned to a platter. Repeat with the remaining chicken pieces.

Add the onions, bell peppers, garlic, cayenne, and curry powder to the skillet and cook until soft, scraping up any browned bits on the bottom of the skillet. Stir in the tomatoes, breaking the tomatoes up into chunks. Return the chicken to the skillet skin-side-up. Reduce the heat, cover, and simmer until the chicken is tender, about 30 minutes. If the sauce is too thick, add a little of the reserved tomato liquid. Cool and season to taste with salt and pepper; add additional cayenne or curry powder, if desired. Remove the chicken, cool, and remove the chicken from the bone. Discard the bones and skins. Return the chicken meat to the cooled sauce.

To serve, bring the chicken and sauce to a boil quickly, stirring frequently. Reduce the heat to low and cook until heated through. Stir the currants or raisins into the sauce, along with any of the optional ingredients as desired. Serve the chicken and sauce over the hot rice. Garnish with the almonds. Serve with chutney, if using, on the side.

This may be made a day or two ahead and refrigerated, covered, or frozen for up to three months, reserving the currants or raisins and optional ingredients until the after the dish is reheated.

Virginia Coq au Vin

The French know their birds. If you are a chicken lover, then you would love visiting a boucherie *in France where you can feast your eyes on all sizes of poultry on display, from the single-serving* poulette *to the fattened (and castrated) rooster called a capon. Traditionally coq au vin was served at home: An earthy, long-cooking braise tenderized the household's tough old rooster. Today coq au vin conjures up dining in a fine French restaurant, far from its peasant roots. In* Mastering the Art of French Cooking, *Julia Child wrote marvelous detailed instructions on how to make this glorious dish, but here I've taken liberties to speed up the process. After all, not many of us have an old rooster on hand! Since our birds today are not tough to begin with, they don't need to braise for hours, but they do need to absorb the wine to honor the traditional flavors of this dish. Marinating does just that.*

Virginia food writer Patrick Evans-Hylton introduced me to Chatham Vineyard's Chatham Creek Vintner's blend, a Bordeaux-style red wine perfect for this recipe (and a glass for the cook too, please). Noted Virginia winemaker Luca Paschina's Barboursville Vineyard's flagship wine, Octagon, is a Bordeaux-style wine that would be perfect to serve with this dish.

I use frozen pearl onions, but feel free to buy fresh and peel them on your own. Julia finished the sauce with 2 tablespoons butter. I've made it optional, but let your culinary conscious be your guide. The sauce is so divine that I encourage serving this dish with buttered noodles to enjoy every last drop.

1 (3½-pound) chicken, cut into 8 pieces
2 cups red wine
8 ounces fresh mushrooms
2 medium carrots
6 pieces bacon
8 ounces frozen pearl onions (or fresh, peeled)
3–4 sprigs fresh thyme
2 garlic cloves, crushed
1 cup chicken stock or broth
2 tablespoons butter (optional)
Buttered noodles (optional)

Place the chicken pieces in a large resealable plastic bag. Add the wine, seal the bag, and let it sit, turning the bag occasionally, while you prepare the other ingredients. Chop the mushrooms and the carrots into roughly ½-inch pieces and set aside.

Cook the bacon in a large Dutch oven or other large ovenproof pot over medium heat until crispy. Remove the bacon to a paper-towel-lined rack or plate. Remove the chicken from the bag (reserving the wine) and pat the pieces dry. Cook the chicken, skin-side-down, in the hot fat from the bacon, in batches if necessary to avoid overcrowding, until the skin is nicely browned, about 5 or so minutes. Turn the pieces over to brown the other side for 3–4 minutes. Remove the chicken to a rack or plate.

Preheat the oven to 350°. Cook the mushrooms in the hot fat for 8–10 minutes, then add the carrots and pearl onions, stirring frequently to brown all sides, about 6–8 more minutes. Chop the bacon and add it to the mushroom mixture; stir in the reserved wine from marinating the chicken, scraping the bottom of the pot to loosen any browned bits. Add the thyme, garlic, and chicken stock or broth and bring to a quick boil, then turn off the heat. Add the browned chicken to the pot, reserving the breast meat pieces. Move the pot to the oven and cook for 45 minutes. Add the chicken breasts to the pot and continue to cook for about 25 minutes, until the thickest part of the thigh reaches 175° and the breasts reach 165° on an instant-read thermometer. Remove the chicken from the pot to a plate. Add the butter, if using, to the sauce. If a thicker sauce is desired, return the pot to the stove and boil until the sauce is reduced in volume and thickens slightly. Return the chicken to the pot, submerge it in the sauce, and serve with buttered noodles, if desired.

Carolina Gold Arroz con Pollo

We call this famous Latin American dish "chicken with rice," but to fully understand this dish, notice that the word for rice comes first. That's where the flavor is in this dish. Numerous versions exist, but this is my favorite since I use Carolina Gold rice (see page 40). Green peas are traditional in this recipe, but I omit them (long story).

MAKES 6–8 SERVINGS

3½ cups chicken broth or stock, divided
3 or 4 strands saffron threads
1 (3½-pound) chicken, cut into 8 pieces
Salt
Freshly ground black pepper
2 tablespoons canola oil
1 large yellow (or Spanish) onion, chopped
1 large green bell pepper, cored, seeded, and chopped
3 ounces chorizo sausage, chopped
2 teaspoons ground cumin
1 teaspoon dried oregano
2 cups Carolina Gold or other medium- or long-grain rice
3 garlic cloves, minced
1 large ripe tomato, chopped
¾ cup drained pimento-stuffed green olives
¼ cup chopped fresh cilantro (optional)
2 limes, cut into wedges, for serving

Place ½ cup of the chicken broth or stock in a small bowl, add the saffron, and leave to soak until needed. Pat the chicken dry and season with salt and pepper. Heat the oil in a large Dutch oven over medium-high heat. Add the chicken pieces skin-side-down, and cook, in batches if necessary to avoid overcrowding, until the skin is nicely browned, about 5 or so minutes. Turn the pieces over to brown the other side for 3–4 minutes. Remove the chicken to a rack or plate.

Add the onion and bell peppers to the hot fat and cook until the onions are soft and lightly browned, about 6–7 minutes. Add the sausage, cumin, and oregano, stirring well to mix, and cook until the sausage is heated through. Stir the rice into the onion and sausage mixture until the rice is well incorporated. Cook for 3–4 minutes, or until the rice just begins to turn translucent around the edges. Stir in the garlic, tomato, and olives and cook for 2 minutes. Pour the remaining chicken stock or broth over the rice mixture and scrape up any browned bits from the bottom of the pot. Bring to a boil, then quickly lower the heat to simmer. Arrange the chicken pieces over the rice (they will be partially submerged in the liquid). Cover and simmer for about 30–35 minutes, checking occasionally to see that the rice is not drying out. If necessary, add ¼ cup additional stock or water. The dish is fully cooked when the rice is tender and has absorbed the liquid and the thickest part of a chicken thigh reaches 175° on an instant-read thermometer. Sprinkle with cilantro, if using, and serve from the pot. Offer the lime wedges to be squeezed on individual portions.

Crispy Fried Chicken

Known as the Gospel bird for its propensity to appear on the Sunday dinner plate, fried chicken is an iconic southern dish. Served around the country at diners and fine dining establishments alike, fried chicken still makes southerners swoon, ex-pats long to return to the southland, and everyone else wish they were here—at least on Sundays.

Southern fried chicken seems basic enough—coat the chicken and fry it up—but even with its variations, it is a technique-driven dish. The traditional vessel is a cast-iron frying pan (12-inch is ideal), but enameled cast iron is also a good choice. It must be heavy and never nonstick. A lid helps to steam-cook the chicken while the first side is browning. It also cuts down on some of the spatter. I'm partial to my large Dutch oven since its high sides keeps most of the spattering oil inside the pan.

For my taste, brining is essential. It is heartbreaking to bite into the glorious, browned coating of fried chicken only to sink your teeth into what seems like Styrofoam. Brining ensures moist, juicy meat as the salt denatures the proteins in the meat so the tightly wound muscle fibers loosen and take on the flavor of the brine. Buttermilk combined with salt is my brine of choice. In an effort to improve on my delicious crust, I experimented with the coating and achieved superior results with dry-wet-dry coating for an extra-crispy crust. Since my grandmother floured her chicken by shaking it in a brown paper bag, I do, too. Be sure to shake off any excess flour as it tends to clump, fall off, and burn on the bottom of the pot. Three resting periods—after brining, after flouring the second time, and after frying—improves results as well. Selecting a frying medium divides cooks into several camps. I grew up on shortening and still use it today. Canola or peanut oil is excellent as well. Lard has many supporters, as does adding a bit of bacon fat to any medium. No matter the choice, Rebecca Lang, author of Fried Chicken *(Ten Speed Press, 2015), and I both agree that the oil should be heated to 325° and monitored closely during cooking to remain between 310° and 325° while the chicken is cooking. It is* customary in recipes to see 350° as the target, but at this temperature, it is easy to burn the crust before the meat is cooked. A clip-on candy/deep-fry thermometer or a high-temperature instant-read thermometer is essential. As with browning chicken in a skillet, overcrowding produces poor results, so fry in batches. I taught my brother-in-law Rob Bare how to fry chicken with this recipe. He upped his game when he added a spoonful of bacon grease to the fat and a tablespoon of smoked ancho chili powder to the second round of flour.

BREADING

Breading is a three-step process to keep your chicken moist while frying and to give each piece the crispy, flavorful crust we love. It's called the dry-wet-dry method, which allows the flour to adhere to the skin of the chicken and builds up a wet layer so the second coating of flour will adhere as well. Although I shake my chicken in a paper bag filled with the flour and/or other dry ingredients, you can bread the way it is usually done, in three shallow bowls or pans. First, dip the chicken in a bowl of flour to coat (and shake off any excess), next dip it in a bowl of lightly beaten egg mixed with whatever additional ingredients are called for (e.g., buttermilk, milk, water), and, finally, dip it in a second bowl of flour, seasoned if desired, or other dry breading mixture (e.g., bread crumbs), shaking off the excess. Place the chicken on a wire rack to allow the coating to settle. To avoid coating your wet hands in the breading, use your right hand for handling the dry coatings and use your left hand for handling the wet coating. When moving the wet chicken to the last dry coating, use your right hand to sprinkle some of the flour over the top of the chicken so your hand will remain dry as you move the chicken to the rack. If you're left-handed, use your left hand to handle the dry coatings.

FOR THE CHICKEN
1 (3½-pound) chicken, cut into 8 pieces
½ cup salt
7 cups buttermilk

FOR THE COATING
4 cups all-purpose flour
1 large egg
1 teaspoon baking powder
½ teaspoon baking soda
1 cup buttermilk

Shortening for frying

Fit two rimmed baking sheets with wire racks and set aside.
Place the chicken pieces in a large resealable plastic bag.
Dissolve the salt in the buttermilk and pour the mixture over
the chicken. Seal the bag and refrigerate for at least 3 hours.
Remove the chicken from the brine and set it on one of
the prepared racks. Return the chicken to the refrigerator,
uncovered, while preparing the coating and oil.

Measure the flour into a large double-thick brown bag.
Whisk the egg, baking powder, baking soda, and buttermilk
together in a large wide bowl. In a heavy skillet or Dutch oven
over medium-high heat, heat enough shortening that when
melted it is 1 inch deep.

Remove the chicken from the refrigerator and add half of
the pieces to the paper bag. Shake to thoroughly coat with flour.

Remove the coated chicken pieces, dip them in the egg mixture, and return them to the bag of flour. Shake again. Remove the chicken pieces, shaking off any excess flour, and return them to the rack. Repeat these steps with the remaining chicken pieces. Let the chicken rest for 10 minutes.

When the melted shortening has reached 325°, add half the chicken pieces, skin-side-down. Cover with a lid and cook for 7–10 minutes. After 4 or 5 minutes, check that the oil is maintaining a temperature of 310–325° and adjust the heat accordingly. At the same time, move any chicken pieces that may be browning too fast to the cooler edges of the pan. After the initial 7–10 minutes of cooking, remove the cover and turn the chicken pieces over. Continue to cook, uncovered, for about 6–7 minutes, or until the chicken is cooked through and the thickest part of the thigh reaches 175° on an instant-read thermometer. Remove the chicken to the second prepared rack and cook the remaining chicken following the same steps above. Serve hot.

VARIATION ✳ SWEET-TEA BRINE For a buttermilk brine alternative, bring two cups of water to a boil in a medium saucepan. Remove from the heat and add 2 (black tea) tea bags. Steep for 7–8 minutes and discard the tea bags. Add 1 cup of granulated sugar and stir until completely dissolved. Let cool 30 minutes. Add ½ cup of salt and stir until dissolved. Add 3 cups of ice cubes and 2 lemons, cut into wedges, to a large nonglass pitcher or pot. Pour the tea over the ice and refrigerate until the tea is thoroughly chilled, about 2–3 hours. When the tea is chilled, move the chicken pieces to a large resealable plastic bag. Pour the tea over the chicken, seal the bag, and refrigerate for at least 6 hours. Continue with the frying directions above.

Ode to the Women of Gordonsville, Virginia

No one knows the recipe used by the waiter-carriers of post–Civil War Gordonsville, Virginia, who sold their fried chicken from large trays balanced on their heads to the passengers on the trains, but I suspect it was similar to the recipe used by the celebrated chef and cookbook author Edna Lewis from Freetown, Virginia, just thirty miles away. Ms. Lewis's grandfather, who was an emancipated slave, obtained his property from a plantation owner, and Edna was raised from birth in this postbellum community of freed people. Fried chicken, made from birds that were hand-fed special food to yield tender, tasty meat, was a special dish served in late spring thru summer. Ms. Lewis fried her chicken in home-rendered lard, freshly churned butter, and a piece of country ham. Given the proximity of Gordonsville to Freetown, I'll bet it's the country ham in the fat that made the Gordonsville chicken so beloved. My recipe is inspired by Ms. Lewis's recipe from The Taste of Country Cooking *and how she makes these ingredients shine.*

MAKES 4–6 SERVINGS

FOR THE CHICKEN

2 (2¼–2½-pound) whole chickens, cut into 8 pieces each, reserving backs

1 celery rib with leaves

1 (¾-inch-thick) slice onion

3 cups cold water

1 cup all-purpose unbleached flour

1 cup whole-wheat flour

3 teaspoons salt

1 teaspoon freshly ground black pepper

½ cup lard, at room temperature

½ cup butter, at room temperature

1 small slice country ham

4 tablespoons fat from pan in which chicken is cooked
3 tablespoons all-purpose unbleached flour
Salt
Freshly ground black pepper

Prepare the stock in advance by simmering the chicken backs, celery, onion, and water in a medium saucepan over medium-high heat. When the stock has begun bubbling vigorously, reduce the heat to a gentle simmer and cook for 1 hour. Pour through a mesh sieve, discarding solids. Leave to cool at room temperature.

Meanwhile, fit two rimmed baking sheets with wire racks and set aside. Measure the flours, salt, and pepper into a large paper bag. Add half of the chicken pieces to the paper bag and shake to thoroughly coat with flour. Remove the chicken pieces, shaking off any excess flour, and transfer them to one of the prepared racks. Repeat these steps with the second half of the chicken pieces, adding them to the same rack. Let rest for 1 hour.

Heat the lard and butter over medium-high heat in a heavy skillet or Dutch oven to 325° and add the country ham and half of the chicken pieces, skin-side-down. Cover with a lid and cook for 7–10 minutes. After 4 or 5 minutes, check that the oil is maintaining a temperature of 310–325° and adjust the heat accordingly. At the same time, move any chicken pieces that may be browning too fast to the cooler edges of the pan. After the initial 10 minutes of cooking, remove the cover and turn the chicken pieces over. Continue to cook, uncovered, for about 6–7 minutes or until you can see that the chicken is cooked through and the thickest part of the thigh reaches 175° on an instant-read thermometer. Remove the chicken to the second prepared rack and cook the remaining chicken following the same steps above.

While the second batch is cooking, prepare the gravy by removing 4 tablespoons of fat from the pan to an 8- or 9-inch skillet. Place the skillet over medium heat and add the flour. Whisk or stir constantly until the flour turns a medium brown, taking care not to burn it. Stir in 2½ cups of the cooled chicken stock and immediately reduce the heat to low. Simmer the gravy for about 15 minutes. It will thicken as it cooks. Season to taste with salt and pepper. If the gravy has become too thick, thin it with a little more stock. Serve hot with the chicken.

VARIATION ✳ MARYLAND FRIED CHICKEN Maryland Fried Chicken is fried chicken served with white gravy. Instead of browning the flour as above, just whisk it into the fat completely and add 1½ cups whole milk instead of chicken stock. Cook until thickened as desired.

Marion Flexner's Fried Chicken with Hardin County Chicken Biscuits

Marion Flexner's cookbook, Out of Kentucky Kitchens, *was first published in 1949 with a preface by Kentucky native and restaurant critic Duncan Hines. Her book became a classic. Her recipe for fried chicken calls for two spring chickens weighing just two pounds each, soaked in milk. If you can obtain birds that small, they do make wonderful fried chicken.*

What I love most about her recipe is she serves the chicken with Hardin County (Fort Knox area) Chicken Biscuits topped with Brown Crumb Gravy. The biscuits are fried in fat, and the gravy takes advantage of any crumbs that may be left in the skillet. A shot of bourbon might be in order here.

MAKES 4–6 SERVINGS

FOR THE CHICKEN

1 (3½-pound) chicken, cut into 8 pieces
1 quart whole milk
2 cups all-purpose flour
2 teaspoons salt
1 teaspoon freshly ground black pepper
Canola oil or shortening for frying

FOR THE BISCUITS

1 cup all-purpose flour
2 teaspoons baking powder
¼ teaspoon salt
2 tablespoons cold butter, cut into ¼-inch cubes
¼ cup whole milk

1 tablespoon all-purpose flour
1 cup whole milk
Salt
Freshly ground black pepper

Place the chicken pieces in a large resealable plastic bag or a deep bowl. Pour the milk over the chicken and let it soak for 20 minutes. When ready to cook, fit a rimmed baking sheet with a wire rack and set aside. Place the flour, salt, and pepper in a large bowl. Preheat the oven to 200°.

Fill a heavy skillet or Dutch oven with oil to a depth of ½ inch and heat to 325°. Dredge half the chicken pieces in the flour, shake off any excess, and place them skin-side-down in the hot oil; cover and cook for 7–10 minutes. After 5 minutes, check that the oil is maintaining a temperature of 310–325° and adjust the heat accordingly. At the same time, move any chicken pieces that may be browning too fast to the cooler edges of the pan. After the initial 10 minutes of cooking, turn the chicken pieces over and continue to cook, uncovered, for about 6–7 minutes, or until the chicken is cooked through and the thickest part of the thigh reaches 175° on an instant-read thermometer. Remove the chicken to the wire rack and move to the oven. Repeat with the remaining chicken. Hold the chicken in warm oven until the biscuits and gravy are ready.

To make the biscuits, sift the flour, baking powder, and salt into a large bowl. Scatter the butter over the flour and use a snapping motion with your fingers to cut the fat into the flour. Add the milk and stir briefly. Turn the dough out onto a floured board. Pat and fold the dough 2 or 3 times and then pat out to ½-inch thickness. Cut the dough into small squares with a pastry wheel, or use a 1–1½-inch biscuit cutter.

Return the fat used for frying the chicken to 325°. Fry the biscuits until they are golden-brown all over, turning if necessary, for a total of 3–4 minutes. Transfer the cooked biscuits to the baking sheet with the chicken in the oven.

To make the gravy, pour off all but 2 tablespoons of the fat in the skillet, but leave any crumbs, and return the skillet to the heat. Sprinkle in the flour and stir constantly until lightly browned, being careful not to burn it. Gradually add the milk, whisking constantly to prevent lumps from forming. Taste and season with salt and pepper. Remove from the heat when the gravy is thickened. Pour into a gravy boat and serve with the hot chicken and biscuits.

Latin Fried Chicken
with Smoky Ketchup

My friend and colleague Sandra Gutierrez is a terrific cook and wonderful cookbook author. This is her recipe, one of the most requested recipes in her cooking classes, from her marvelous book The New Southern-Latino Table: Recipes the Bring together the Bold and Beloved Flavors of Latin America and the American South. *She uses a larger chicken (5 to 5½ pounds) that is first fried, then moved to a hot oven to finish cooking, creating a crunchy exterior. This cooking method prevents the spices and flour from burning and allows excess fat to render out. The result is chicken that is moist but not greasy. Made this way, chicken can be kept in a warm oven for a full hour before serving without becoming soggy. Her secret to a crunchy crust is to use self-rising flour instead of all-purpose flour.*

MAKES 4–6 SERVINGS

FOR THE CHICKEN

1½ cups buttermilk

¼ cup minced cilantro (leaves and tender stems)

2 tablespoons minced chipotle chiles in adobo

1 teaspoon adobo sauce (from the canned chipotles)

½ teaspoon garlic powder

1 teaspoon salt

Pinch of freshly ground black pepper

1 chicken (5–5 ½ pounds), cut into 10 serving pieces

3 cups self-rising flour

2 teaspoons paprika

1½ teaspoons salt

1 teaspoon ground coriander

1 teaspoon garlic powder

1 teaspoon cayenne pepper

1 teaspoon ancho chile powder

½ teaspoon freshly ground black pepper

Vegetable oil for frying (about 4–5 cups)

1½ cups ketchup
2 tablespoons chipotle chiles in adobo,
    chopped to a fine paste
1 teaspoon adobo sauce
2 teaspoons ancho chile powder

Combine the buttermilk, cilantro, chipotle, adobo sauce, garlic powder, salt, and pepper in a large bowl. Add the chicken and toss to coat; cover and chill for at least 6 hours (or up to 24).

When ready to cook, preheat the oven to 325°. Fit two baking pans with metal cooling racks. In a large bowl, combine the flour, paprika, salt, coriander, garlic powder, cayenne, chile powder, and pepper. Dredge the chicken in the flour mixture and set on one of the prepared racks. Let the chicken dry for 5 minutes. In a large Dutch oven, heat 3½ inches of oil to 360°. Working in batches, dredge the chicken in the flour mixture a second time, shaking off any excess flour; fry the white meat for 8 minutes and the dark meat for 10 minutes, or until the crust is crispy and reddish-brown. Transfer the fried chicken to the other prepared rack. Bake for 20–25 minutes, or until an instant-read thermometer inserted into the thigh of the chicken registers between 180° and 185° (the juices will run clear when the chicken is pierced with a fork). To keep the chicken warm (up to 1 hour), reduce the oven temperature to 250°.

In a small bowl, combine the ketchup, chipotle, adobo sauce, and chile powder; chill until ready to use. The smoky ketchup will keep, covered tightly, for up to 1 week in the refrigerator. Serve chicken hot, with smoky ketchup.

Asha Gomez's Kerala Fried Chicken with Mango Drizzle

Asha Gomez is an Atlanta chef who has married her coastal Indian roots with her home in the American South. She built her culinary reputation with her restaurant Cardamom Hill with regulars begging for more of her Kerala Fried Chicken. After closing Cardamom Hill, she opened Spice to Table, an Indian pastry shop. Her devotees flock to the Old Fourth Ward in Atlanta at 11 a.m. on Fridays and Saturdays for her famous fried chicken. Don't be late . . . it's available only until it runs out. If you aren't one of the lucky ones in line, here is her recipe, along with her Mango Drizzle. Asha recommends using kesar or alphonso mangos, found at Indian grocery stores. This dish marinates overnight.

MAKES 4–6 SERVINGS

FOR THE DRIZZLE

½ cup mango pulp
4 Thai green chiles
2 garlic cloves
¼ teaspoon salt
1 teaspoon granulated sugar

FOR THE CHICKEN

2 cups buttermilk
10 garlic cloves
1 (2-inch) piece fresh ginger, peeled
6 whole serrano peppers (seeded, if desired)
1 cup fresh cilantro
1 cup fresh mint
2 tablespoons kosher salt
8 bone-in, skin-on chicken thighs
4 cups all-purpose flour

2 tablespoons coconut oil
Shortening for frying
2 stems curry leaves for garnish (optional)

Purée the mango pulp, chiles, garlic, salt, and sugar for the mango drizzle in a food processor or blender. Set aside.

Purée the buttermilk, garlic, ginger, peppers, cilantro, mint, and salt in a blender or food processor. Place the chicken in a large resealable plastic bag. Pour the buttermilk mixture over the chicken, seal the bag, and refrigerate for 24 hours.

When ready to cook, fit two rimmed baking sheets with wire racks and set aside. Remove the chicken from the brine and set it on one of the prepared racks. Measure the flour into a large bowl. Melt the coconut oil over low heat in a small pan and leave to simmer.

In a heavy skillet or Dutch oven over medium-high heat, heat enough shortening that when melted it is ½ inch deep. When the oil has reached 325°, dredge half of the chicken pieces in the flour, shaking off any excess flour, transfer them, skin-side-down, to the hot oil, and cook for 7–10 minutes. After 5 minutes, check that the oil is maintaining a temperature of 310–325° and adjust the heat accordingly. At the same time, move any chicken pieces that may be browning too fast to the cooler edges of the pan. After the initial 10 minutes of cooking, turn the chicken pieces over and continue to cook for about 6–7 minutes, or until the chicken is cooked through and the thickest part of the thigh reaches 175° on an instant-read thermometer. Remove the chicken to the second prepared rack and baste with the simmering coconut oil. Cook the remaining chicken following the same steps above. Fry the curry leaves, if using, just until crisp, about 10–15 seconds. Serve the chicken with the Mango Drizzle and garnish with the curry leaves.

Bourbon Barbecued Chicken

Entire books are written about barbecue and the succulent meats coated with sauce from old family recipes and grilled to perfection. Grilled chicken always says summer to me, and I love how the meat stays moist inside while the skin blisters and chars to perfection. I offer my humble recipe to you as a place to start. By thinning the sauce, you can build up layers while avoiding large flare-ups from thickly dripping sauce. But keep a spray bottle of water on hand just in case!

MAKES 4–6 SERVINGS

2 cups ketchup

½ cup fresh lemon juice

¼ cup white or cider vinegar

¼ cup light or dark brown sugar

¼ cup honey

2 tablespoons Worcestershire sauce

2 teaspoons dry mustard

1 teaspoon onion powder

1 teaspoon garlic powder

1 cup bourbon

1 (3½-pound) chicken, cut into 8 pieces

Stir the ketchup, lemon juice, vinegar, sugar, honey, Worcestershire sauce, mustard, onion and garlic powders, and bourbon together in a medium saucepan over medium heat. When the sauce begins to bubble, reduce the heat to low and simmer until you are ready to grill the chicken, stirring occasionally. When ready to cook, pour half the sauce into a container for basting the chicken outside on the grill. Thin it with water (up to ½ cup) as needed. Reserve the remaining sauce for serving with the chicken.

Prepare the grill to medium-high heat on one half of the grill and low heat on the other half. Baste the chicken with the thinned sauce and place it skin-side-down on the hot side of grill. Grill for 5–6 minutes on each side over the direct heat, basting once halfway through. Move the chicken to the indirect heat and continue to grill, basting several times during cooking, until the thickest part of the breast reaches 165° and the thickest part of the thigh reaches 175° on an instant-read thermometer. Discard the basting sauce. Remove the chicken to a platter and serve hot with the reserved sauce.

Nashville Hot Chicken

Nashville is the epicenter for hot chicken. And by hot I mean fiery-burn-your-mouth-spicy hot. Prince's, Bolton's, and Hattie B's restaurants have all garnered national attention over the last few years for their blistering crispy creations. I'm a bit of coward in this arena, so I developed this recipe with a glass of milk by my plate! The good news is you can control the heat and adjust the seasonings to become your own fire-breathing dragon. Increase the amount of cayenne to your tolerance, but this is pretty hot.

The heat builds from the ground up, beginning with cayenne in the buttermilk brine and the hot sauce added to the egg wash. But the key to the sensational heat is in the lard-based sauce that is brushed over the chicken as it comes out of the skillet, just like they do in Nashville.

Some chicken shacks deep fry the chicken and some are still cooking in skillets. I'm using the dry, wet, dry method so the extra-crispy crust will hold up to the hot glaze. Note that this is a twenty-four-hour marinade.

MAKES 4–6 SERVINGS

FOR THE CHICKEN

3 cups buttermilk

¼ cup cayenne pepper

½ cup garlic powder

¼ cup onion powder

½ cup paprika

2 tablespoons granulated sugar

1 (3½-pound) chicken, cut into 8 pieces

2 cups all-purpose flour

2 large eggs

1 cup milk or buttermilk

1 tablespoon Louisiana-made hot sauce,
   such as Frank's or Tabasco

FOR THE FINISHING SAUCE

½ cup lard

3 tablespoons cayenne pepper

1 tablespoon light or dark brown sugar

1 teaspoon paprika

1 teaspoon salt

1 teaspoon freshly ground black pepper

Shortening, for frying

White bread, for serving

Slice pickles, for garnish

Stir together the buttermilk, cayenne, garlic powder, onion
powder, paprika, and sugar in a large bowl. Place the chicken
in a large resealable plastic bag and pour the buttermilk mixture
over the chicken. Seal the bag, turn to coat the chicken, and
refrigerate for 24 hours.

When ready to cook, fit two rimmed baking sheets with wire
racks and set aside. Remove the chicken from brine and set on
one of the prepared racks.

Measure the flour into a large double-thick brown bag.
Whisk the eggs, milk or buttermilk, and hot sauce together in a
large wide bowl.

Melt the lard over low heat and whisk in the cayenne, brown
sugar, paprika, salt, and pepper and leave to simmer.

Heat enough shortening in a large heavy skillet or Dutch
oven so that when melted it is 1 inch deep. Add half of the

chicken pieces to the paper bag. Shake to thoroughly coat with flour. Remove the coated chicken pieces, dip them in the egg mixture, and return them to the bag of flour. Shake again. Remove the chicken pieces, shaking off any excess flour, and return them to the rack. Repeat these steps with the remaining chicken pieces.

When the oil has reached 325°, add half the chicken pieces, skin-side-down, and cook, covered, for 7–10 minutes. After 5 minutes, check that the oil is maintaining a temperature of 310–325° and adjust the heat accordingly. At the same time, move any chicken pieces that may be browning too fast to the cooler edges of the pan. After the initial 7–10 minutes of cooking, turn the chicken pieces over and continue to cook for about 6–7 minutes, or until the chicken is cooked through and the thickest part of the thigh reaches 175° on an instant-read thermometer. Remove the chicken to the second prepared rack and baste with the simmering sauce. Cook the remaining chicken following the same steps above. Serve the chicken hot on two slices of white bread and garnish with sliced pickles as they do in Nashville.

What's Your Favorite Piece?

When a platter of chicken is set down at the table, and they're all your favorite pieces of chicken, all is right with the world. You eat leisurely knowing you won't have to fight anyone for another piece, as you might if it were a whole cut-up chicken.

Why are we so fond of these all-of-one packages of chicken? For one thing, when the rise of the healthy white-meat banner was unfurled regaling chicken breasts as the answer to our diet woes in the 1970s, packages of breast-only chicken took over the cold case. As new cooks entered the market with little apron-string kitchen knowledge, fewer people were cutting up their own chicken. Now the boneless chicken breast is ubiquitous. If breasts are your favorite part of the chicken and you want avoid overcooking them, look to recipes that poach the breast in liquid, brine it before cooking, or are served with sauce. Pickle-Brined Fried Chicken Sandwiches, Chicken Parmesan Patti, and Stephanie's Picnic Chicken all fit the bill.

Chicken thighs are my particular favorite. Roasted, baked, or broiled, the flavorful and nutritious dark meat stays moist. Chicken Thighs with Fennel and Lemon and Bourbon-Peach Chicken Thighs will prove the point.

Chicken wings are served all over the country broiled or fried. Try Hoisin-Sauced SEC Wings and Korean Twice-Fried Chicken Wings to taste the difference.

And let's not leave out the chicken livers. Fried with bacon or chilled in pâté, chicken livers are equally at home with mashed potatoes for a family meal or served with celebratory champagne.

Substitute your favorite part of the bird in any of these recipes, adjusting the cooking time accordingly to cook thighs or legs to an internal temperature of 175° and chicken breasts to 165°.

Cynthia's Honey Mustard Chicken Thighs

For years I have served this dish to family and friends, particularly on holidays when I serve more than one meat entrée for a large crowd. It insures that the picky eaters—both children and adults—will have something to eat, especially if I'm serving a lamb or pork roast, or a rare beef tenderloin. Marinating the thighs a few hours or overnight is the key to infusing the fullest flavor from the honey and mustard. Consider adding 2–4 teaspoons curry powder to the marinade as a variation. Serve with plain white rice, or any favorite grain, to soak up the tangy, sweet juices in the pan.

MAKES 6–8 SERVINGS

½ cup honey
2 tablespoons Dijon mustard
2 tablespoons whole or coarse-grain mustard
8 bone-in, skin-on chicken thighs
Salt
Freshly ground black pepper
Cooked rice (optional)

Stir together the honey and both mustards in a small bowl. Place the chicken thighs in a large resealable plastic bag. Pour the honey mixture over the chicken, seal the bag, turn to coat the chicken evenly, and refrigerate for several hours or overnight.

When ready to cook, preheat the oven to 350°. Remove the thighs to a 9 × 13-inch baking dish or pan and discard the excess marinade. Season with salt and pepper. Bake for 50 minutes, or until the thickest part of a chicken reaches 175° on an instant-read thermometer. Serve over rice, if desired, along with the pan juices.

Chicken Thighs with Fennel and Lemon

There are practically no words to describe this dish. The aroma in the kitchen while it bakes is heavenly. The fennel bulb and fennel seed bring out an even meatier taste in the chicken. The mustard provides a smooth tang and ups the earthy taste of the thighs. The pan juices are divine, so I serve this dish with rice, or at least crusty bread for dipping.

Marinating this dish one hour or overnight enhances the flavors, but it isn't entirely necessary for a tasty dish. To prepare the fennel bulb, cut off any long stalks growing from the bulb and discard them, but reserve a tablespoon of chopped feather fronds to top the finished dish, if desired.

MAKES 6–8 SERVINGS

¼ cup fresh lemon juice

2 tablespoons whole-grain mustard

2 tablespoons chopped fresh tarragon

1 tablespoon fennel seed

1 teaspoon salt

½ teaspoon freshly ground black pepper

⅓ cup olive oil

2 fennel bulbs, cut into 6 or 8 wedges each

8 bone-in, skin-on chicken thighs

2 tablespoons light or dark brown sugar

½ cup dry white wine

2 lemons, thinly sliced

1 tablespoon chopped fennel fronds (optional)

Combine the lemon juice, mustard, tarragon, fennel seed, salt, and pepper in a medium bowl. Slowly whisk in the oil to emulsify the marinade. Transfer the marinade to a large resealable plastic bag. Add the fennel and chicken thighs, seal the bag, and turn to coat with the marinade. Refrigerator for at least 1 hour or overnight.

When ready to cook, preheat the oven to 350°. Transfer the chicken to one or two large, shallow baking dishes or pans so the chicken rests in a single layer. Scatter the fennel wedges around the chicken. Pour the excess marinade evenly over the chicken.

Stir together the sugar and wine in a small bowl and pour the mixture over the chicken. Arrange the lemon slices around the pan. Bake for 50 minutes to 1 hour, or until the thickest part of a chicken thigh reaches 175° on an instant-read thermometer. Transfer the chicken and fennel to a serving platter. Tent with foil to keep warm. Pour the sauce from the baking dish(es) into a small saucepan and bring to a boil. Reduce the heat to low and cook until the sauce is reduced in volume by about half; pour it over the chicken. Top the finished dish with fennel fronds, if using, and serve hot.

Lessie Clifton's
Yellow Mustard Chicken Thighs

My sweet friend Kellie Meckes shared this recipe belonging to her grandmother, Lessie Clifton of Douglas, Georgia. I've just about decided the best recipe from any great country cook begins with chicken, and this is no exception. And of course the very best recipes are handed down from one generation to the next, as this one has with Lessie having given it to her daughter Lois, and now it's Kellie's turn to keep it alive. Yellow ballpark mustard is the star here. I was tempted to make it with Dijon, but the yellow mustard is a pleasant, slightly tangy surprise.

This is what I call a pantry meal—one that I always have the ingredients on hand for.

MAKES 4–6 SERVINGS

---

8 bone-in, skin-on chicken thighs

$\frac{1}{2}$ teaspoon salt

$\frac{1}{4}$ teaspoon freshly ground black pepper

$\frac{1}{2}$ teaspoon garlic powder

Canola oil for frying

3 tablespoons fresh lemon juice

3 tablespoons yellow mustard

Water or dry white wine, if needed for sauce

Pat the chicken dry. Sprinkle with the salt, pepper, and garlic powder. Heat ½ inch of oil in a large skillet or Dutch oven over medium heat. In batches if necessary to avoid overcrowding the pan, cook the chicken pieces skin-side-down until golden brown, about 5 or so minutes. Turn the pieces over to brown the other side for 3–4 minutes. Remove the chicken as it is browned to a platter. When all the thighs are browned, return them to the pan. Pour the lemon juice over the chicken. Using a basting brush (I use a silicone one), coat the chicken with the mustard. Cover, reduce the heat to low, and cook for about 45 minutes, or until the thickest part of the thigh reaches 175° on an instant-read thermometer. Remove the chicken to a platter and assess the sauce. If needed, add water or wine, 1 tablespoon at a time, until the sauce is thinned enough to drizzle over the chicken. Serve hot.

Summertime Anytime
Bourbon Peach Chicken Thighs

I always feel like a traitor to my state (Georgia) when I eat South Carolina peaches and feel like South Carolina should be the peach state. I wish fresh peach season would never end, and I always look for new ways to use them, especially in savory dishes. I even unabashedly use frozen peaches in the off season. Freestone peaches are the easiest to use, but sliced cling peaches are nearly as easy. And frozen peaches also work well here. The minced shallot is superb in this dish, but a Vidalia or other sweet onion could be substituted for a milder flavor. The bourbon is a mild taste in this dish—not at all overpowering. The bourbon brand is your call. Aren't we fortunate to have so many to choose from?

MAKES 6–8 SERVINGS

---

8 bone-in, skin-on chicken thighs
Salt
Freshly ground black pepper
2 tablespoons canola oil
1 shallot, finely minced
⅓ cup bourbon
4 sprigs fresh rosemary
3 peaches, peeled, pitted, and sliced

Preheat the oven to 350°. Pat the chicken dry. Season with salt and pepper. Heat the oil in a large oven-proof skillet or Dutch oven over medium-high heat. Working in batches if necessary to avoid overcrowding, cook the chicken pieces skin-side-down until golden brown, about 5 or so minutes. Turn the pieces over to brown the other side for 3–4 minutes. Remove the chicken to a platter (the chicken will not be fully cooked at this point). Drain off all but 2 tablespoons of the fat in the pan. Cook the shallots in the hot fat, scraping up any browned bits on the bottom of the pan. Stir in the bourbon and scrape again if needed. Return the chicken to the pan. Tuck the rosemary springs in between the thighs and scatter the peaches over the thighs. Cover and bake for 45 minutes to 1 hour, or until the thickest part of a chicken thigh reaches 175° on an instant-read thermometer. Transfer the chicken and peaches to a serving dish and discard the rosemary. Coat the chicken lightly with the pan juices. If any juices remain, pour them into a gravy boat and serve with the chicken.

Chicken Marbella

The Silver Palate Cookbook *(Workman, 1982), written by Julee Rosso and Sheila Lukins, is filled with creative recipes that changed what American hostesses put on their dining tables, especially for company. Recipes for marinated goat cheese, pesto, salmon with dill sauce, flourless chocolate torte, and this dish—with its assertive flavors of the Mediterranean through the generous amount of garlic, oregano, and olive oil—first appeared to the masses in the pages of this celebrated and award-winning cookbook. You'll find the recipe for Chicken Marbella all over the internet with comments such as "my aunt used to make this recipe and she gave it to me" and variations on this theme, with no mention of the iconic cookbook that brought it to the national stage. Here it is as a salute to the genius cookbook authors that invented it.*

The bay plant in my garden was about a foot tall when I made this recipe for the first time. It is now a substantial tree more than fifteen tall. Snipping the fresh leaves to use in this recipe is always a treat. I never make less than the recipe calls for and am happy to have the leftovers for another night or to freeze for later. It also doubles easily to serve a crowd.

6 garlic cloves, chopped
1/4 cup dried oregano
1 teaspoon salt
1/2 teaspoon freshly ground black pepper
1/2 cup red wine vinegar
1/2 cup olive oil
1 (12-ounce) package bite-size pitted prunes
1 (7-ounce) jar pitted Spanish green olives, drained
1 (3 1/2-ounce) jar capers, drained
6 whole bay leaves, fresh or dried
8 bone-in, skin-on chicken thighs
1/2 cup light or dark brown sugar
1 cup dry white wine

Stir together the garlic, oregano, salt, pepper, and vinegar in a medium bowl. Whisk in the olive oil to emulsify. Add the prunes, olives, capers, and bay leaves, stirring well to mix. Transfer the mixture to a large resealable plastic bag. Add the chicken thighs, seal the bag, and refrigerate for several hours or overnight.

When ready to cook, preheat the oven to 350°. Transfer the chicken to one or two large, shallow baking dishes or pans. Pour the excess marinade evenly over the chicken.

Stir together the sugar and wine in a small bowl and pour the mixture over the chicken. Bake for 50 minutes to 1 hour, or until the thickest part of a chicken thigh reaches 175° on an instant-read thermometer. Turn the heat to broil, if needed, to crisp the chicken skin. Remove the chicken from the oven and transfer it, along with the prunes, olives, and capers, to a serving platter. Remove the bay leaves. Coat lightly with the pan juices. Pour the remaining juices into a gravy boat and serve with the chicken.

Roasted Chicken Thighs
with Muscadines

Native to the American South, muscadines and their sister grapes, scuppernongs, have been cultivated since Native American times. Early southern settlers used them to make wine and put them in pies and jellies. Roasting muscadines, or any other grape, mellows any sharpness to them and concentrates their flavor. Here they are nestled next to chicken with shallots and Kalamata olives—a savory and juicy combination. The muscadines are thick-skinned. Cut them in half lengthwise and use the tip of a sharp knife to remove the seeds. You can substitute red or green seedless grapes as desired. Red or white wine may be substituted for ½ cup of the chicken stock at the end. Serve this dish with crusty bread to sop up the luscious juices.

MAKES 6–8 SERVINGS

8 bone-in, skin-on chicken thighs
2–3 tablespoons olive or canola oil
Salt
Freshly ground black pepper
1 pound muscadines, halved and seeded, or red or green
    grapes, cut from the large stems into small clusters
1 shallot, minced
½ cup pitted Kalamata olives
½ cup chicken stock or broth

Preheat the oven to 350°. Pat the chicken thighs dry and move them to one or two large, shallow baking dishes or pans where they can rest in a single layer. Brush the skin with the oil and season with salt and pepper. Scatter the muscadines or grape clusters, shallot, and olives around the chicken. Pour the chicken stock or broth into the pan.

Bake the chicken for 50 minutes to 1 hour, or until the thickest part of a chicken thigh reaches 175° on an instant-read thermometer. Turn the heat to broil, if needed, to crisp the chicken skin. Remove the chicken from the oven and transfer it, along with the muscadines or grapes and olives, to a platter. Coat lightly with the pan juices. Pour the remaining pan juices into a saucepan over medium-high heat. Let the juices reduce for 5 or so minutes, pour them into a gravy boat, and serve with the chicken.

Aunty Elizabeth's Chicken Paprikash
Paprikás Csirke

Hungary is known for its dishes featuring paprika, a spice made of ground roasted peppers, and its most well-known chicken dish is Paprikás Csirke, a stew with chicken (csirke). Paprika ranges in flavor from sweet to hot, depending on the blend of sweet red peppers used. The most common imported blend available here is édesnemes, a bright red, slightly sharp paprika usually labeled sweet paprika. Do purchase a Hungarian brand—it is the most flavorful.

This recipe comes from my dear friend Andrea Pell, who was a young ballet student in Budapest in the 1970s. Her housemother, who Andrea adoringly called "Aunty Elizabeth," kept a large ham hung on a hook suspended from the low ceiling of her walk-in pantry. Over time, the ham dripped lard into a chipped enamel bowl that sat atop an old wooden stool. Within the thick, cool masonry walls of the pantry, behind its massive wooden door, the lard cooled to become soft and creamy. It was this lard that she used to start her Sunday "paprikás." Aunty Elizabeth never put sour cream in her paprikash, so I don't either.

The chicken in this dish falls from the bone, so set the table with shallow bowls, forks, and spoons. Buttered noodles should line the bowls before serving, and thick slices of rustic bread are mandatory to sop up the rich gravy. Consider serving a creamy cucumber salad as an accompaniment.

2 tablespoons canola oil or fresh lard, if available
1 small onion, diced
1 medium green bell pepper, cored, seeded, and diced
1 medium red bell pepper, cored, seeded, and diced
1 medium tomato, diced
2 tablespoons tomato paste
$\frac{1}{2}$ teaspoon kosher salt
$\frac{1}{4}$ teaspoon freshly ground black pepper
2 tablespoons Hungarian sweet paprika
$\frac{1}{2}$ teaspoon cayenne pepper (optional)
8 bone-in, skin-on chicken thighs
Buttered noodles, for serving

Heat the oil or lard in a large Dutch oven over medium-high heat. Add the onion and cook until softened, about 5–6 minutes. Reduce the heat to low, add the green and red bell peppers, and cook for 10 minutes, stirring occasionally. Stir in the tomatoes, tomato paste, salt, pepper, paprika, and cayenne, if using. Pat the chicken pieces dry and add to the pot. Cover and continue cooking over low heat for about 45 minutes, or until the thickest part of the thigh reaches 175° on an instant-read thermometer. Turn the chicken over halfway through cooking time and stir the sauce. Serve hot on a bed of buttered noodles. *Jó étvágyat* (good appetite)!

Skillet Turmeric Chicken Thighs

When recent studies suggested turmeric, with its anti-inflammatory and antioxidant properties, might play a role in cognitive brain health, I jumped on the bandwagon and added more of it to my cooking. Turmeric is a member of the ginger family and is common in South Asian and Middle Eastern cooking, adding beautiful color and it's slightly bitter taste to traditional dishes. Here it is simply rubbed on the chicken before braising.

MAKES 4–6 SERVINGS

8 bone-in, skin-on chicken thighs

2 teaspoons ground turmeric

1½ teaspoons salt

½ teaspoon freshly ground black pepper

2 tablespoons canola oil

1 shallot, minced

4 garlic cloves, finely chopped

1 cup dry white wine

2 teaspoons chopped fresh tarragon

2 limes, cut into wedges (optional)

Pat the chicken dry. Combine the turmeric, salt, and pepper in a small bowl and rub the mixture on the chicken pieces. Heat the oil in a large skillet or Dutch oven over medium-high heat. Cook the chicken pieces, in batches if necessary to avoid overcrowding, skin-side-down, until golden brown, about 5 or so minutes. Turn the pieces over to brown the other side for 3–4 minutes. Remove the chicken to a platter. Add the shallot and garlic to pan and cook 1–2 minutes. Stir in the wine, scraping up any browned bits on the bottom of the pan, and heat until bubbly. Return all the chicken to the pan. Cover, reduce the heat to low, and cook for about 30 minutes. Sprinkle the tarragon over the chicken and cook, uncovered, an additional 15 or so minutes, or until the thickest part of the thigh reaches 175° on an instant-read thermometer. Remove the chicken to a platter and bring the sauce to a boil. Reduce the heat to low and simmer the sauce until slightly thickened. Serve the chicken with the sauce and the lime wedges, if desired.

Butter Chicken
Chicken Makhani

Full-flavored and fragrant, Chicken Makhani hails from Delhi, India, and is a staple in Indian restaurants. Redolent with ginger, turmeric, and garam masala, the overnight marinade transforms the chicken. The dish is finished with a tomato cream sauce, which has a stick of butter in it. How bad could it be?

MAKES 4–6 SERVINGS

3 garlic gloves, peeled
2 tablespoons chopped fresh ginger
2 teaspoons ground turmeric
2 tablespoons garam masala
2 tablespoons ground cumin
Juice of 1 lemon
1 cup plain Greek yogurt
8 bone-in, skin-on chicken thighs, skins removed
1/2 cup butter
2 medium onions, chopped
1 jalapeño pepper, stemmed, seeded, and finely chopped
1 (14-ounce) can diced tomatoes, or 1 large ripe tomato, chopped
1 tablespoon tomato paste
1 cup heavy cream
1/2 cup fresh cilantro leaves (optional)
Cooked rice, for serving

Pulse together the garlic, ginger, turmeric, garam masala, and cumin in the bowl of a food processor to chop the garlic finely. Add the lemon juice and yogurt and pulse until combined. Transfer the yogurt mixture to a large resealable plastic bag. Add the chicken, seal the bag, and turn to coat with the marinade. Refrigerate for several hours or overnight.

When ready to cook, melt the butter in a large skillet over medium heat. Add the onions and jalapeño and cook until the onion is soft and translucent, about 5 minutes. Add the tomatoes and their liquid, stir, and cook 2–3 minutes, or until the tomatoes are heated through. Add the chicken and marinade to the pan, stir, and reduce the heat to low. Simmer the chicken for about 30 minutes. Combine the tomato paste and cream in a small bowl and stir into the chicken. Cook for 15 more minutes, or until the thickest part of the thigh reaches 175° on an instant-read thermometer. Top with cilantro, if using. Serve with rice.

Sheet Pan Chicken Thighs and Sweet Potatoes

April McGreger, author of the Sweet Potatoes *volume of this series, is an authority on sweet potatoes, having grown up on her family's sweet potato farm. Even though I'm not the expert she is, we both know how the sweet potato is transformed when baked in the oven and the caramel-like sugars melt and the flesh becomes so soft it's practically self-mashed. The sweet potato wedges in this recipe are cut ¾-inch thick to be fully cooked at the same time as the chicken. Larger wedges will need more time.*

The simplicity of cooking two or three dinner items on the same sheet pan is just irresistible to me, and Molly Gilbert's Sheet Pan Suppers *has provided much inspiration to me. Just a salad will round out this meal.*

MAKES 4–6 SERVINGS

½ cup olive oil
¼ cup red wine vinegar
1 teaspoon salt
½ teaspoon freshly ground black pepper
½ teaspoon dried oregano
½ teaspoon dried basil
2 large sweet potatoes
8 bone-in, skin-on chicken thighs

Preheat the oven to 350°. Line a sheet pan with aluminum foil and set aside. Whisk the oil into the vinegar in a large wide bowl to emulsify. Stir in the salt, pepper, oregano, and basil. If desired, peel the potatoes (I don't peel). Cut them lengthwise into ¾-inch-thick wedges, add them to the oil mixture, and toss to coat. Transfer the potatoes to half of the prepared sheet pan. Add the chicken to the bowl and toss with the remaining oil mixture. Transfer the chicken, skin-side-up, to the other half of the pan.

Bake for 50–60 minutes, turning the potato wedges once or twice during cooking. The chicken is cooked when the thickest part of a thigh reaches 175° on an instant-read thermometer. Serve hot.

Chicken Thighs with Charleston Ginger-Pear Chutney

The pineapple has been the symbol of Charleston hospitality since they arrived in her port in the early eighteenth century, and chutneys have been in the South since the colonies were formed. Even early southern cookbooks contain recipes for chutney. Marinating boneless thighs in pear chutney and pineapple juice for at least one hour or overnight yields very tender, juicy meat, and this recipe has been a go-to family favorite for a very long time. There are many types of chutneys, and most any would be appropriate here. When I'm not making my own, I commonly use Major Grey's, which is found on the condiment aisle of a regular grocery store. It's a blend of mangos, raisins, sugar, and spices, and it's thick like jam. Although this recipe is written for the broiler, these marinated thighs are easily grilled over medium heat, for about 5–6 minutes per side.

MAKES 6–8 SERVINGS

FOR THE CHUTNEY

1 small shallot, minced

1 teaspoon canola oil

2 ripe pears, cored, seeded, and finely diced

$\frac{1}{4}$ cup cider vinegar

1 teaspoon grated fresh ginger

3 tablespoons honey

$\frac{1}{4}$ cup raisins

FOR THE CHICKEN

$\frac{1}{3}$ cup pineapple juice

$\frac{1}{3}$ cup soy sauce or tamari

1 garlic clove, minced

$\frac{1}{4}$ cup canola oil

2 pounds boneless, skinless chicken thighs

To make the chutney, sauté the shallots over medium heat in a saucepan drizzled with the oil. Add the pears, vinegar, ginger, and honey and bring to a boil. Reduce the heat and cook until the pears are tender, about 5 minutes. Remove from the heat and stir in the raisins. Let sit to cool for 10–15 minutes before using.

To make the chicken, combine ½ cup of the pear chutney with the pineapple juice, soy sauce or tamari, garlic, and oil in a blender and blend until smooth. Pour the mixture into a large resealable plastic bag. Add the chicken thighs, shake the bag to coat, and refrigerate for at least 1 hour or overnight.

When ready to cook, preheat the broiler. Line a broiler pan with foil (for easy clean up) and remove the thighs from the marinade with tongs to the pan. Discard the marinade. Broil for 5–6 minutes; turn the thighs over and cook for 5–6 minutes more, or until the thickest part of the thigh registers 175° on an instant-read thermometer. Serve with the remaining chutney at the table, if desired.

New-Fashioned Chicken Divan

My mother, Kathleen Cahill Stevens, was the reigning queen of can-of-soup casseroles in every suburb we lived in around this country. Bless her heart, as we say. Although I broke out of the can-of-soup mold by the time I had graduated from college, Chicken Divan remained in my heart as a comfort food dish.
To square with my modern sensibilities, I rehabbed this recipe to eliminate the can of soup. My dear friend, fellow southerner, and consummate food writer and storyteller Sheri Castle was my houseguest on the night I tested this recipe. We discovered that we both love dry mustard and think it's terribly underrated, so feel free to add more than this recipe calls for if you are a fan as well. The sliced, toasted, and buttered white bread is essential.

MAKES 4 SERVINGS

Canola oil or cooking spray
4 slices white bread
6 tablespoons butter, divided
3 cups broccoli florets
4 cups chicken stock or broth
2 boneless, skinless chicken breasts (about 1½ pounds)
½ cup all-purpose flour
1½ cups whole milk
2–3 tablespoons dry sherry
1 tablespoon dry mustard
Pinch nutmeg or 1 tablespoon curry powder
Salt
Freshly ground black pepper
1 cup grated cheddar cheese
½ cup grated Parmesan cheese

Preheat the oven to 350°. Oil or spray an 8 x 8-inch baking dish and set aside. Toast the bread and spread with 2 tablespoons of the butter. Cut it into 1-inch squares and set aside. Steam the broccoli florets for 3–4 minutes, rinse them under cold water, and set them in a colander to drain until needed.

In a medium stockpot, bring the chicken stock or broth to a boil over medium-high heat. Add the chicken and reduce the heat to low; cover and simmer the chicken for 15–18 minutes. Remove the chicken to a cutting board and let the stock cool. Cut the chicken into bite-size pieces.

Melt the remaining butter in a saucepan over medium-low heat. Whisk in the flour and stir briefly to incorporate it into the butter, about 1 minute. Stir in 2 cups of the stock from cooking the chicken. Whisk constantly until smooth. Whisk in the milk and reduce the heat to a simmer. Continue whisking until smooth, about 1–2 minutes. Continue cooking the sauce, stirring occasionally, until thickened. Stir in the sherry, mustard, and nutmeg or curry powder, season with salt and pepper, and remove from the heat.

Coat the bottom of the prepared dish with a third of the sauce. Scatter half of the broccoli florets over the sauce. Scatter half of the chopped chicken over the broccoli. Sprinkle with half of the cheddar cheese. Pour another third of the sauce over the cheese. Repeat with another layer, pouring the remaining sauce over the chicken. Sprinkle with the Parmesan cheese and top with the toast squares. Bake for 35–45 minutes, or until bubbly. Serve hot.

Grilled Jamaican Jerk Chicken Breasts

I met the lovely Helen Willinsky just after her first book, Jerk: Barbecue from Jamaica, *was published. Through her recipes she brought to life the addictive Caribbean grilled meats available at huts dotting the island roads. I think Helen will approve of my version of this recipe. Marinating the chicken at least six hours or overnight infuses the chicken with quintessential Jamaican flavor. The Scotch bonnet pepper is traditional, but you can substitute a pepper you know. If you are a little heat-averse, use just a small portion of the pepper. I like to serve this with rice and sliced fresh mango to cool the palate from the jerk seasonings.*

MAKES 4 SERVINGS

4 boneless, skinless chicken breasts
2 tablespoons soy sauce
1 tablespoon white or cider vinegar
2 teaspoons granulated sugar
1 teaspoon freshly ground black pepper
1 teaspoon ground allspice
½ teaspoon ground cinnamon
½ teaspoon ground nutmeg
1 Scotch Bonnet pepper, cored, seeded, and chopped
1 teaspoon chopped fresh ginger
1 tablespoon canola oil

Flatten the chicken breasts between two sheets of wax paper to ½ inch thick and place them in a large resealable plastic bag.

Place the soy sauce, vinegar, sugar, black pepper, allspice, cinnamon, nutmeg, Scotch Bonnet pepper, ginger, and oil in the bowl of a food processor. Pulse to combine and chop the pepper fine. Pour the marinade over the chicken, seal the bag, and refrigerate for at least 6 hours or overnight.

When ready to cook, heat the grill to medium-high heat on one half of the grill and low on the other half. Place the chicken on the hot side of the grill. Grill for 4–5 minutes on each side, basting once during that cooking time. Discard the leftover marinade. Move the chicken to the cooler side and continue to grill until the thickest part of the breast reaches 165°. Serve hot.

Pickle-Brined
Fried Chicken Sandwiches

We have a venerable fast-food institution in the South known as Chick-fil-A. It has gained renown for its chicken sandwich: golden fried chicken breast served on a steamed hamburger bun with only two slices of dill pickle to adorn the sacred sandwich. Truett Cathay, its founder, kept his restaurants closed on Sundays in light of religious observance, leaving legions of fried chicken sandwich addicts adrift one day a week. Cooks have tried to achieve the same flavors at home, but remain second-rate to Cathay's esteemed fried boneless breast. Although variations abound, it is clear to me that the chicken breasts are pickle-brined. Here is my experiment reminiscent of the lauded sandwich. I save the juice from two jars of dill pickles to make the brine.

2 boneless, skinless chicken breasts
2 cups dill pickle juice
4 soft hamburger buns
2 tablespoons butter, melted
8 dill pickle slices
1 large egg
1 teaspoon baking powder
½ teaspoon baking soda
1 cup buttermilk
2 cups of all-purpose flour
2 teaspoons paprika
½ teaspoon freshly ground black pepper
½ teaspoon garlic powder
½ teaspoon onion powder
½ teaspoon Italian seasoning
¼–½ teaspoon cayenne pepper
Canola oil or shortening for frying

Flatten the chicken breasts between two sheets of wax paper to ½ inch thick. Cut each breast into two roughly equal pieces. Move the chicken pieces to a large resealable plastic bag. Pour the pickle juice over the chicken, seal the bag, and refrigerate for 2–4 hours.

When ready to cook, fit two rimmed baking sheets with wire racks and set aside. Open the hamburger buns and coat the inside of each with the melted butter and place them on one of the prepared racks. Lay two pickle slices on one side of each bun. Remove the breasts from the brine and place them on the second prepared rack.

Whisk the egg, baking powder, baking soda, and buttermilk together in a large wide bowl. Whisk together the flour, paprika, pepper, garlic powder, onion powder, Italian seasoning, and cayenne in a separate large wide bowl.

Fill a heavy skillet or Dutch oven with oil to a depth of 1 inch (or with enough shortening that when melted it is 1 inch deep). Pat the chicken dry with paper towels. Dip each piece into the egg wash to coat, then dredge in the flour mixture. Shake off excess and return to the rack.

When the oil has reached 325°, cook the chicken breasts, in batches if necessary to avoid overcrowding, for 5–6 minutes per side, or until the chicken is cooked through and the thickest part of a breast reaches 165° on an instant-read thermometer. Remove the chicken to the prepared rack to drain briefly, then move to the prepared buns. Cover with a sheet of aluminum foil to steam-heat the buns. Serve hot.

Chicken Parmesan Patti

White-tablecloth dining was a very special occasion growing up, and my favorite restaurant as a child while visiting with my grandparents in Jacksonville, Florida, was Patti's Italian Restaurant on Beach Boulevard, just a few blocks from my grandparents' home in Kilarney Shores. Established in 1951 by Peter and Mary Patti when Beach Boulevard was still unpaved, it was one of the first restaurants in Jacksonville to spotlight Italian cuisine. Patti's closed in 1994 but the memory of its boneless chicken parmesan lives on. The Jacksonville Times-Union *printed several of Patti's most popular dishes over the years, and my efforts here closely match my taste memory from years ago. Use this sauce recipe in other of your favorite Italian dishes—it's a keeper. If pushed for time, use your favorite bottled red sauce instead. Chicken breasts are so large these days that when I purchased a package of six for this recipe, it was clearly enough for ten, if not twelve, people. The number of breasts you'll need will depend on the size you purchase.*

And yes, there's no parmesan in this recipe. As Peter Patti's grandson John said in an interview in 2001, "We left out the parmesan. That's what put us on the map."

FOR THE SAUCE

4 (10-ounce) cans tomato purée
2 (6-ounce) cans tomato paste
2 tablespoons garlic powder
2 tablespoons dried basil
1 teaspoon dried oregano
3 tablespoons granulated sugar
3 teaspoons salt
1 teaspoon freshly ground pepper
3 cups water

FOR THE CHICKEN

2 cups all-purpose flour
$\frac{1}{2}$ teaspoon dried oregano
$\frac{1}{2}$ teaspoon salt
$\frac{1}{4}$ teaspoon freshly ground black pepper
2 large eggs
$\frac{1}{2}$ cup water or milk
2 cups panko bread crumbs
6 boneless, skinless chicken breasts
4–6 tablespoons canola or olive oil, divided
$\frac{1}{2}$ cup finely grated Romano cheese
12 thin slices provolone cheese

To make the sauce, combine the tomato purée, tomato paste, garlic powder, basil, oregano, sugar, salt, pepper, and water in a large heavy pot. Simmer on low for 4 hours, stirring occasionally. The sauce may be refrigerated for several days or frozen for up to 3 months. Thin with additional water as needed before use.

To make the chicken, fit a large rimmed baking sheet with a wire rack and set aside. Select a baking dish large enough to hold the chicken in a single layer or just slightly overlapping. Coat the bottom of the dish with a third of the sauce and set aside.

Whisk together the flour, oregano, salt, and pepper in a large bowl and set aside. Whisk together the eggs and water or milk in a separate large bowl. Spread the panko out on a plate. Flatten the chicken breasts between two sheets of wax paper to about ¾ inch thick. Cut each breast in half and pat dry. Dredge the breasts in the flour, dip them in the egg mixture, pat them into the bread crumbs, and move them to the prepared rack.

Heat 2 tablespoons of the oil in a large heavy skillet over medium-high heat. Working in batches, adding additional oil as needed to the pan, cook the chicken breasts for 7–8 minutes; turn them over and cook for another 7–8 minutes, or until the interior of the breast reaches 165° on an instant-read thermometer. Remove the chicken breasts to the sauced baking dish. Cover lightly with sauce. Preheat the broiler.

Dust the chicken with the Romano cheese and cover each piece with a slice of the provolone cheese. Broil just long enough for the cheese to bubble and brown ever so lightly. Serve hot.

VARIATION ✳ CHICKEN MEATBALLS Instead of Chicken Parmesan, make a batch of meatballs to go with the sauce above. In a large bowl mix together ¼ cup plain bread crumbs, ¼ cup chopped parsley, 2 large beaten eggs, 1 tablespoon milk, 1 tablespoon ketchup, ¾ cup grated Romano cheese, and ¾ teaspoon each salt and pepper. Add 1 pound ground chicken and stir to combine. Roll the mixture into ¾-inch balls. Heat 1 tablespoon of canola oil in a large heavy skillet. Add the meatballs and cook for 2 minutes; turn the meatballs over and brown the other side for 2 minutes. Remove to the warm sauce and serve over pasta.

Fried Chicken and Waffles

Although the Pilgrims introduced waffles to the New World in the 1600s in what became Pennsylvania Dutch country, it wasn't until Thomas Jefferson returned from a trip to France with a waffle iron after the French Revolution that waffles became more widely known. And it was in the kitchens of the antebellum southern plantations that the "Virginia Breakfast," consisting of fried or baked meats with some kind of quick bread, from biscuits to cornbread to waffles, became popular. Adrian Miller, food writer and soul food scholar, writes about the history of chicken and waffles in his book Soul Food: The Surprising Story of An American Cuisine *(2013, UNC Press): "After Emancipation, [freed] cooks frequently made chicken and waffles for social events in the black community and as professional cooks in elite hotels, resorts, and restaurants patronized by wealthy whites." In popular lore, Joe Wells served chicken and waffles in the 1930s at his Harlem night club, satisfying the late-night/early-morning hunger of his clientele. Roscoe's Chicken and Waffles in Los Angeles began serving the dish in the 1970s and now has locations all across the city. I use boneless chicken breasts for ease of eating a bite of both the chicken and the waffle at the same time.*

1 recipe Crispy Fried Chicken (page 54),
    using 4–6 boneless chicken breasts
1¾ cups all-purpose flour
2 teaspoons baking powder
2 teaspoons baking soda
1 teaspoon granulated sugar (optional)
1½ cups buttermilk
3 large eggs
½ cup butter, melted and cooled, plus more for serving
Honey, for serving (optional)

Preheat the waffle iron. Whisk the flour, baking powder, baking soda, and sugar, if using, together in a large bowl. Beat together the buttermilk, eggs, and melted butter in another bowl. Pour the egg mixture into the flour mixture and stir well to combine. Cook the waffles in the waffle iron according to the manufacturer's directions. Serve the waffles spread with butter and a piece of fried chicken on top. Drizzle with honey, if desired.

Stephanie's Picnic Chicken Tenders

Stephanie Delaney was my neighbor last summer when I was in Maine. She was stretching her culinary wings, and I was the lucky recipient of her many triumphs. When she shared this fried boneless chicken, I knew I had to have the recipe. Although it's delicious hot, this is the perfect fried chicken to tote for a picnic because the taste of the seasoning still remains after chilling. Fried chicken aficionados, including John T. Edge, author of Fried Chicken: An American Story, *claim that in order to call chicken fried, it must have a bone, and I had agreed. Until I tasted Stephanie's.*

MAKES 6 SERVINGS

2 pounds chicken breast tenderloins

1 quart buttermilk

2½ cups all-purpose flour

2 cups panko bread crumbs

1½ tablespoons Lawry's seasoning salt

1 teaspoon garlic powder

Freshly ground black pepper

3 tablespoons Grill Masters Montreal Chicken Seasoning

2 large eggs

Canola or other oil for frying

Pat the chicken dry and place it in a large resealable plastic bag. Add all but 2 tablespoons of the buttermilk and refrigerate for at least 6 hours or overnight. Reserve the remaining buttermilk.

When ready to cook, remove the chicken from the refrigerator and let it come to near room temperature while you prepare the other ingredients. Fit two rimmed baking sheets with wire racks and set aside. Stir the flour, bread crumbs, and seasonings together in a large bowl. Place ¾ cup of the mixture in a large plate and place the remainder in a large plastic bag. Lightly beat the egg and the remaining buttermilk together in a medium bowl. Dredge each piece of chicken in the flour mixture, shaking off the excess, then dip in the egg mixture. Place half of the chicken in the bag with the flour mixture and shake to cover evenly. Remove the chicken with tongs, shaking off any excess flour mixture, to the prepared rack. Repeat with remaining chicken. Let rest for 10 minutes.

Fill a heavy skillet or Dutch oven with oil to a depth of 1–1½ inches and heat it to 325°. Fry the breasts, two at a time, very gently turning with tongs, until the internal temperature of the chicken reaches 165° on an instant-read thermometer. As the chicken is cooked, remove it to the second prepared rack. Serve hot or leave to cool, then refrigerate loosely covered with wax paper. Keep it cold until serving.

Sautéed Chicken Tenders
with Mississippi Comeback Sauce

A Greek restaurant in 1930s Jackson, Mississippi, is credited with the invention of the comeback sauce—a sauce you'll surely come back to once you've had it. Originally used as the house salad dressing, it's now found a home next to all manner of fried foods, from chicken, fish, and shrimp to fried green tomatoes and fried pickles, as a dipping sauce, which is how it's used here. Its addictive flavor is a cross between that of a Russian dressing and a thousand island dressing.

These chicken tenders benefit from the two-hour brining time, but if you're in a hurry, I'll understand.

MAKES 2–4 SERVINGS

---

10 chicken breast tenderloins
2 tablespoons salt
1 cup buttermilk
Freshly ground black pepper
1 cup Duke's mayonnaise
½ cup olive oil
⅓ cup chili sauce
¼ cup ketchup
1½ tablespoons Worcestershire sauce
2 teaspoons freshly ground black pepper
⅛ teaspoon paprika
1 medium onion, finely chopped
2 garlic cloves, minced
1 tablespoon vegetable oil

Pat the chicken dry and place it in a large resealable plastic bag. In a small bowl, stir the salt into the buttermilk until dissolved. Pour the mixture over the chicken and refrigerate for at least 2 hours or overnight.

For the sauce, stir together the mayonnaise, olive oil, chili sauce, ketchup, Worcestershire sauce, pepper, paprika, onion, and garlic in a small bowl and refrigerate.

When ready to cook, remove the sauce from the refigerator and set aside. Heat the vegetable oil in a heavy skillet over medium-high heat. Add the chicken and cook a total of 8–12 minutes, turning halfway through the cooking time with tongs, until the internal temperature of the chicken reaches 165° on an instant-read thermometer. Serve hot, with sauce.

White Chicken Chili

White chili is a nice change of pace from its traditional red, tomato-based cousin. My dear friend Catherine Fliegel makes this version, which is chock-full of vegetables and fabulous flavor. If you really need some heat, add 1 teaspoon cayenne pepper. Serve the chili with plenty of blue corn tortilla chips.

MAKES 4–6 SERVINGS

1 tablespoon olive oil
1 pound chicken breast tenderloins
1 medium onion, chopped
1 medium yellow bell pepper, cored, seeded, and chopped
2 garlic cloves, minced
2 teaspoons ground cumin
1 teaspoon salt
½ teaspoon freshly ground black pepper
1 cup fresh or frozen corn kernels
1 (15-ounce) can cream-style corn
1 (4.5-ounce) can mild chopped green chiles
1 (15-ounce) can small white beans, rinsed and drained
2 cups milk
1 cup shredded white cheddar cheese, plus extra for topping
    (optional)
Diced avocado, for garnish (optional)
Salsa verde (green salsa) with or without jalapeños (optional)

Heat the oil in a large Dutch oven over medium heat. Pat the chicken dry and add it to the oil. Stir in the onion, bell pepper, and garlic. Cover and cook for 4 minutes; turn the chicken over, cover, and cook for 4 minutes more. Remove just the chicken to a cutting board and cover with aluminum foil.

Stir the cumin, salt, and pepper into the vegetables and cook for 2 minutes, or until the cumin is fragrant. Add the corn, chiles, beans, and milk, stirring well to combine. Increase the heat to medium-high and bring the mixture to a boil. Reduce the heat to low, cover, and simmer for 10 minutes, stirring occasionally.

Shred the chicken and add it to the pot and stir. Cook for 5 minutes, or until the chicken is heated through. Add the cheese and stir until melted.

Top individual portions with extra cheese, diced avocado, and salsa verde, if desired.

Korean Twice-Fried Chicken Wings

Korean fried chicken has soared in popularity here in the United States, showing up on bar menus and at chicken joints in major cities. The spicy chili paste called gojujang, found in Asian markets, is the secret to the addicting heat. We Atlantans are lucky to have a large neighborhood of Asian restaurants and grocers to choose from on Buford Highway.

Double frying yields the delectable crackly crust that is the hallmark of this dish. Achieving the irresistible crust at home is tricky when cooking a whole cut-up chicken, but I find chicken wings cook up perfectly. After cutting the tips from the wings, cut the flat from the drum at the joint if desired. Rice flour and cornstarch aid in achieving a crispy crust.

MAKES 4 SERVINGS

---

5 garlic cloves, peeled
2-inch piece fresh ginger, peeled
4 tablespoons soy sauce
4 tablespoons gojujang
2 tablespoons fresh lime juice
2 tablespoons rice vinegar
1 tablespoon dark sesame oil
2 tablespoons honey
⅓ cup rice flour
⅓ cup all-purpose flour
⅓ cup cornstarch
1 cup water
2 pounds chicken wings, tips removed
Canola oil or shortening for frying

Pulse the garlic and ginger together in a food processor until chopped finely. Add the soy sauce, gojujang, lime juice, vinegar, oil, and honey and pulse to combine. Pour into a small saucepan and simmer over low heat until ready to serve.

Fit two rimmed baking sheets with wire racks and set aside. Whisk together the rice flour, all-purpose flour, and cornstarch in a medium bowl. Add the water and stir well to combine. Add the chicken and coat thoroughly. Remove the chicken to one of the prepared racks.

Fill a heavy skillet or Dutch oven with oil to a depth of 1½ inches (or enough shortening that when melted is a 1½ inches deep) and heat to 325°.

Add half of the chicken pieces to the hot fat and cook until golden brown, about 6–8 minutes, turning with tongs as needed to brown evenly. Remove to the second prepared rack. Repeat with remaining half. Return the oil to 325° and fry each batch a second time, about 6–8 minutes. After draining on racks again, toss the chicken with the warm sauce and serve.

Buffalo Wings

Buffalo, New York, claims Buffalo wings as its own since the spicy wings were first served at the Anchor Bar there in 1964. As legend would have it, when a delivery of chicken wings appeared unexpectedly in place of the usual chicken backs the restaurant needed for the house spaghetti sauce, the owner's wife, Teressa Bellissimo, broiled up the wings for a snack and served them with hot sauce. She later switched to frying the wings, the sauce was thickened with butter, and the finished wings were served with blue cheese and celery sticks. It is a rare gathering for the big game that doesn't feast on a batch of these.

MAKES 4 APPETIZER SERVINGS

½ cup butter
1 cup Louisiana-made hot sauce, such as Frank's or Tabasco
2 tablespoons white vinegar
2 pounds chicken wings, tips removed and separated
   at the joint
Salt
Freshly ground black pepper
Canola oil or shortening for frying
Celery sticks
Blue cheese dressing

Melt the butter with the hot sauce and vinegar in a saucepan over low heat.

Fit a rimmed baking sheet with a wire rack and set aside. Season the wings with salt and pepper. Fill a large Dutch oven with oil to a depth of 1½ inches (or enough shortening that when melted is a 1½ inches deep) and heat to 325° over medium-high heat. Add half the wings to the hot oil and cook for 7–8 minutes, turning occasionally. Remove the wings to the prepared rack. Brush the wings with the hot sauce, coating all sides. Repeat with the remaining wings. Serve with celery sticks and blue cheese dressing for dipping.

Hoisin-Sauced SEC Wings

These are my family's favorite wings—perfectly sticky and finger-licking good. Hoisin is one of those magic ingredients—it's both salty and a little sweet, in a way like barbecue sauce. It's thick and dark and glazes the wings beautifully. These are a Southeastern Conference game-day regular for us.

MAKES 4–6 SERVINGS

---

3 pounds chicken wings
½ cup hoisin sauce
3 tablespoons soy sauce
Juice of 1 lime
2 teaspoons finely chopped fresh ginger

Preheat the broiler. Line a rimmed baking sheet with aluminum foil and fit it with a wire rack. Set aside. Remove the tips from the wings and discard. Divide each wing into two pieces by cutting through the joint. Pat the wings dry and move to a large bowl. Stir together the hoisin, soy sauce, lime juice, and ginger in a small bowl. Pour the sauce over the chicken and stir well to coat evenly. Transfer the wings to the prepared rack. Broil about 3 inches from the heat for 10 minutes on each side, or until cooked through and glistening, basting halfway through the cooking time. Serve hot.

Nana Stuffie's Fried Chicken Livers

My grandmother made the best fried chicken livers. If there was bacon frying in the evening, it usually meant there would be chicken livers to follow. She pan fried her chicken livers in the fat left behind cooking eight or so slices of bacon. The aroma filled her small two-bedroom house in Jacksonville, Florida, in no time. It was one of my mother's favorite dishes. Substitute canola oil for the bacon if you must. I serve these as an accompaniment to fried chicken or as an appetizer, serving about 3 chicken livers per person.

MAKES 4–6 SIDE-DISH OR APPETIZER SERVINGS

1 pound chicken livers
1 cup milk
2 cups all-purpose flour
2 teaspoons salt
1 teaspoon freshly ground black pepper
8 slices bacon

Trim any larger pieces of fat or sinew from the livers. Move them to a bowl, cover with the milk, and let sit for 1 hour. Whisk together the flour, salt, and pepper and set aside. Cook the bacon in a frying pan over medium heat and remove the cooked pieces to a plate lined with paper towels, reserving the fat in the pan.

When ready to cook the livers, heat the bacon fat over medium heat. Remove the livers from the milk, dredge them in the flour, shaking off any excess, and add them to the hot fat, cooking in batches if necessary to avoid overcrowding the pan. Cook for 5–6 minutes, turning occasionally, until lightly browned on all sides. Remove to a plate lined with paper towels. Serve the hot livers with crumbled bacon.

Fort Washington Avenue Chicken Liver Paté

When my husband was growing up near Fort Tryon Park in New York City, his mother cooked dinner every night to be served shortly after his father walked in the door. She would keep watch at the kitchen window, waiting for Sigmund to exit the 190th Street Station from the A train. Once he appeared, she would set out the "forshpeis," a little nosh before the meal. Her addictive chicken liver paté was a staple. I think of her every time I make it.

MAKES 2 CUPS

1 tablespoon canola or other oil
1 medium onion, sliced
1 pound chicken livers
⅓ cup Madeira or port
2 hard-boiled eggs
2 tablespoons chicken fat (schmaltz)
½ teaspoon salt
¼ teaspoon freshly ground black pepper
3 or 4 lettuce leaves
Crackers, for serving

Heat the oil in a large skillet over low heat. Add the onion and cook, stirring occasionally, until it just begins to turn brown. Remove the onion to the bowl of a food processor. Add the chicken livers and port to the skillet and cook for 5–7 minutes, turning the livers until lightly browned and the liquid has reduced. Add the cooked livers and their liquid, along with the eggs, chicken fat, salt, and pepper, to the onions and pulse several times until smooth, scraping down the sides of the bowl if necessary. Scoop the liver mixture into an oiled serving bowl or mold and refrigerate for at least 2 hours. When ready to serve, scoop or unmold the chopped liver onto the lettuce leaves on a platter. Serve with the crackers.

Chicken Sausages and Apples

This quick skillet dinner is for those days when you simply can't think of what to serve. Look for a high-quality brand of chicken sausage—most brands come with delicious seasonings and are fully cooked.

MAKES 4 SERVINGS

2 tablespoons butter
4 chicken sausages, fully cooked
1 medium onion, sliced
1 medium apple, cored and sliced
¼ white wine
1 cup half-and-half
Spaghetti noodles, if desired

Melt the butter over medium-high heat in a medium skillet. Brown the sausages on all sides, about 5 minutes. Remove the sausages to a plate. Add the onions to the skillet and sauté until soft and lightly browned, about 5 minutes. Add the apples and cook 3–4 minutes, or until the apples are cooked but still firm. Add the wine and scrape any browned bits from the bottom of the skillet. Allow the wine to reduce for about 3 minutes. Slowly pour in the half-and-half. Return the sausage to the pan and cook for 1–2 minutes more. Serve over pasta, if desired.

A Bird in the Hand

COOKED CHICKEN ON HAND
SAVES THE DAY

Cooked chicken on hand brings a meal to the table in record time. From pies, to salads, to soups, there are so many ways to let chicken shine. Biscuit-Topped Chicken Pot Pies are an easy weeknight meal, and Memorable Matzoh Ball Soup is sure to cure what ails you. Every cuisine offers a use for cooked chicken, and even a small amount of leftovers from a roast chicken can come back to the table in a whole new way.

Chicken Sandwich Salad

Chicken salad has always been one of my favorite sandwich fillings, but I'm rarely pleased with it when ordering in a restaurant or sandwich shop. While I think the mayonnaise is essential, I don't want my salad filling dripping out of my sandwich. Walnuts and red grapes are my preferred enhancements to the standard recipe, but the other options listed are delicious as well.

MAKES 4–6 SERVINGS

---

3 cups chopped cooked chicken

2 celery ribs, finely chopped

½ small onion, minced

½ chopped walnuts or pecans or slivered almonds

1½ cups seedless red or green grapes, cut in half

¼ cup Duke's mayonnaise, plus more if desired

¼ cup sour cream or plain yogurt

Salt

Freshly ground black pepper

Toss the chicken, celery, onion, nuts, and grapes in a large bowl. Stir together the mayonnaise and sour cream or yogurt in a small bowl and mix into the chicken mixture. If it's too dry, add additional mayonnaise as desired. Season to taste with salt and pepper. Serve on lettuce leaves, sandwich bread, or rolls.

Biscuit-Topped Chicken Pot Pies

The fresher and more deliciously cooked the chicken, the better the pot pie, but we do not have to go so far as the cook in the nursery rhyme who arranged for "four and twenty blackbirds baked in a pie" and found that "when the pie was opened the birds began to sing." I usually use a store-bought rotisserie chicken for this recipe unless I have cooked chicken on hand from another meal. The biscuit tops are delightful.

MAKES 4 SERVINGS

---

1 cup sliced carrots

2 tablespoons butter

1 cup chopped onion

8 ounces fresh mushrooms, quartered

1 cup frozen cut pole beans, thawed

3 tablespoons all-purpose flour

1 teaspoon kosher salt

¼ teaspoon freshly ground black pepper

1½ cups chicken stock or broth

2 cups shredded or diced cooked chicken

1 cup self-rising flour

½ cup heavy whipping cream

Preheat the oven to 325°. Place four (10-ounce) ovenproof ramekins or bowls on a rimmed baking sheet; set aside.

Place the carrots and 2 tablespoons of water in a microwave-safe glass bowl and microwave on high for 1–2 minutes, or until crisp-tender, and drain. Melt the butter in a medium skillet over medium-high heat. Add the onion and cook for 2 minutes. Add the mushrooms and cook, stirring constantly, for 2 minutes. Add the beans and carrots, and cook for 2 minutes.

Sprinkle the all-purpose flour, salt, and pepper over the vegetables. Cook, stirring constantly, for 1 minute, or until the flour is incorporated. Gradually stir in the stock or broth and cook over medium-high heat, stirring constantly, for 8–10 minutes, or until the mixture is thickened and bubbly. Stir in the chicken and remove from the heat.

Stir together the self-rising flour and cream in a bowl just until flour is moistened. Turn the dough out onto a lightly floured surface. Pat out and fold the dough 3–4 times and then pat it out to ½-inch thickness. Using a 3-inch round cutter, cut out 4 disks, reshaping the scraps once, if necessary, for the fourth biscuit. (Avoid twisting the cutter so the biscuit will rise properly.)

Divide the hot chicken mixture evenly between the prepared ramekins or bowls and top each with the cut biscuit dough. Bake for 20 minutes, or until biscuits are golden brown. Serve hot.

Chicken and Parslied Dumplings

A rich broth and feather-light dumplings provide warmth for both body and soul, and variations abound — use any combination of vegetables you desire. To liven up the dumplings, omit the parsley and use 1 tablespoon freshly ground black pepper.

MAKES 8 SERVINGS

FOR THE CHICKEN
1 tablespoon canola oil
1 medium carrot, diced
1 celery rib, diced
1 small onion, chopped
2 tablespoons all-purpose flour
$\frac{1}{2}$ teaspoon salt
$\frac{1}{4}$ teaspoon freshly ground black pepper
4 cups chicken stock or broth
2 cups diced cooked chicken

FOR THE DUMPLINGS
$\frac{1}{2}$ cup heavy cream, plus more if needed
1 cup self-rising flour
3 tablespoons chopped fresh parsley or thyme

Heat the oil in a large Dutch oven over medium heat. Stir in the carrot and celery and cook 2–3 minutes. Add the onion and cook, stirring occasionally, 5–6 minutes, or until the onion is translucent and the vegetables are softened. Sprinkle the vegetables with the flour and stir until the flour is incorporated and no white spots remain. Stir in the salt and pepper. Add the stock or broth and cook, stirring, until the soup thickens slightly, about 5 minutes. Stir in the chicken. Reduce the heat to low.

In a medium bowl, combine the heavy cream, flour, and 1 tablespoon of the parsley or thyme, to form a wet, sticky dough, adding additional cream as needed. Pinch off tablespoon-size portions of the dough and drop them into the simmering chicken and broth. Cover and simmer 10–12 minutes, or until the dumplings are soft and weepy but cooked through. Ladle the chicken and dumplings into bowls and top with the remaining parsley or thyme.

Doctored Chicken Broth

"I'm 66 years old, and I've never made stock at home in my life," said Andre Soltner, the legendary chef of Lutece for thirty-four years, in an interview with the New York Times. *"The same is true of most chefs, although they won't admit it." It's wonderful to know that even the best chefs might use canned chicken broth at home.*

If you want to use canned broth rather than homemade in a recipe, you can improve the flavor by adding a few ingredients and cooking it for just 20 minutes. It's little extra effort for a lot of taste.

MAKES 1 QUART

1 (32-ounce) carton chicken broth
1 medium onion, unpeeled and roughly chopped
1 medium carrot, roughly chopped
8–10 parsley stems
5 whole peppercorns
Salt, if needed
Freshly ground black pepper, if needed

Bring the broth, onion, carrot, parsley, and peppercorns to barely a boil in a pot over medium-high heat. Reduce the heat to low and simmer for 10–20 minutes. Strain the stock through a fine-mesh strainer or a colander lined with dampened cheesecloth into another pot, pressing the solids to release all of the juices and extract their flavor. Taste and season with salt and pepper, if desired.

Memorable Matzoh Ball Soup

My cousin Anne Graubart, a convert to Judaism as a bride, is known among our relatives in Texas as having made the very best matzoh ball soup on her first attempt. Many years ago, with her new family gathered around, she put on her first Passover Seder— and served her magnificent soup. Her light and fluffy matzoh balls captivated every diner. When she was asked what she had done to make them so special, she replied that she did not have any schmaltz on hand, so she used bacon fat. Thankfully, no one was irrevocably insulted, and some, in years hence, have secretly yearned for her original version. Schmaltz is rendered chicken fat and can be the fat you've removed from homemade chicken stock, rendered by cooking raw chicken fat trimmed from a fresh chicken, or purchased in a jar.

I share here my version which my father-in-law Sigmund said were the kind of matzoh balls he loved—fluffy and tender—and he looked forward to them every time I said they were on the menu. For Anne's memorable version, substitute chilled bacon fat for the schmaltz.

If the uncooked matzoh balls are refrigerated for longer than 15 minutes, they will cook up hard, and be known as "sinkers," rather than these lovely "floaters."

FOR THE SOUP BASE

12 cups water

2–3 pounds chicken wings

2 medium onions, quartered

2 medium carrots, roughly chopped

1 celery rib, roughly chopped

Salt

12 whole black peppercorns

2 cups shredded chicken (optional)

2 medium carrots, sliced (optional)

FOR THE MATZOH BALLS

4 large eggs

¼ cup seltzer

¼ cup schmaltz or canola oil

1 cup matzoh meal

½ teaspoon baking powder

1 teaspoon salt

½ teaspoon freshly ground black pepper

6 cups water

To make the soup base, pour the water into a large pot and add the chicken wings, onion, carrot, celery, salt, and peppercorns; bring to barely a boil over high heat. Reduce the heat to low and simmer for 3 hours, skimming off and discarding any rising fat or foam during the first 30 minutes. Strain the stock through a fine-mesh strainer or a colander lined with dampened cheesecloth, pressing the solids to release all of the juices and extract their flavor. If you're making the soup base ahead of time, cool it and refrigerate for several hours or overnight. When it's cold, skim off the fat that has risen to the surface. Otherwise, return it to the pot, bring it to a simmer, and add the shredded chicken and sliced carrots, if using. Continue to simmer while you make the matzoh balls.

Whisk together the eggs, seltzer, and schmaltz or canola oil in a large bowl. In a separate bowl, stir together the matzoh meal, baking powder, salt, and pepper. Stir the matzoh meal mixture into the wet ingredients. Refrigerate for 15 minutes. While waiting, bring the water to a boil in a large pot with a lid.

Remove the matzoh ball dough from the refrigerator. Using damp hands, roll a heaping tablespoon of the dough into a ball and move to a plate. Working swiftly, continue until all the dough is used. Move all the balls to the simmering water, stir gently, cover, and cook until they are cooked through, about 30 minutes. Remove the matzoh balls from the water with a slotted spoon to the simmering soup. Serve hot. If you are preparing the balls ahead, remove them to a large plastic storage container, cool, then seal tight and refrigerate for up to two days.

Greek Lemon Chicken Soup
Avgolemono

One of the best food festivals in Atlanta is the Greek Festival, which has been taking place for more than forty years. Offering Greek fare ranging from gyro sandwiches to souvlaki to baklava and so much more, it is a feast complete with music, dancing, and singing. For those who can't stay for the fun, they offer a drive-thru menu to satisfy your craving. It's a taste extravaganza, and it inspires many attendees to investigate Greek cuisine at home. This dish is a Greek comfort food classic.

The Greek term for this creamy but light chicken soup, avgolemono, translates literally as "egg and lemon soup." The smooth, thickened broth is enhanced with a spike of lemon juice, and versions are found in Turkey, Albania, Tunisia, and Lebanon.

MAKES 4 SERVINGS

---

2 teaspoons olive oil

1 small onion, chopped

3 garlic cloves, minced

6 cups chicken stock

½ cup uncooked long-grain rice

1 large egg, lightly beaten

⅓ cup fresh lemon juice

2 teaspoons cornstarch

½ teaspoon salt

½ teaspoon freshly ground black pepper

2 cups shredded cooked chicken breast

2 tablespoons chopped fresh parsley

2 tablespoons chopped fresh basil

Heat the oil in a Dutch oven over medium-high heat. Add the onion and garlic and cook for 2 minutes. Add the chicken stock and bring to a boil. Stir in the rice, cover, reduce the heat to low, and simmer for 15 minutes. Lightly whisk together the egg, lemon juice, cornstarch, salt, and pepper in a small bowl. Stirring constantly, slowly add a spoonful of the stock. Now drizzle the egg mixture into the stock, whisking constantly until incorporated. Add the chicken and simmer until the soup thickens and the rice is done, about 3 minutes. Add the parsley and basil just before serving.

Chicken Stock

I save the wing tips discarded from making one of the wing recipes and the backs from whole chickens that I've cut up in plastic bags in the freezer. When I need to make stock, I use whatever I've stored in the freezer and supplement this from the store if need be, usually with chicken wings. After straining, the stock may be reduced by continuing to simmer, yielding a richer stock.

Roasting the chicken and/or bones and vegetables on the stovetop or in a baking pan in the oven until they are deep brown will yield beautiful brown stock. Deglaze the baking pan with a little water, scraping up the browned bits, and add it to the stockpot along with the roasted bones.

MAKES 2 QUARTS

4 pounds chicken bones and/or meat

1 medium onion, quartered

1–2 carrots, roughly sliced

1 celery rib, roughly sliced (no leaves)

4–6 sprigs thyme (optional)

8 parsley stems (optional)

2 garlic cloves, unpeeled (optional)

12 black peppercorns

1 bay leaf

Roughly chop the meat and chop or break up the chicken bones and place them in a large stockpot. Add the onion, carrots, and celery, plus any of the optional ingredients. Add enough water to cover by 4 inches. Bring the mixture to nearly a boil, then reduce the heat and simmer for about 45 minutes. Skim off and discard any rising fat or foam and add the peppercorns and bay leaf. Cover the pan halfway and simmer for 3 hours, stirring occasionally and adding hot water as necessary to keep the bones and vegetables covered. Strain the stock through a fine-mesh strainer or a colander lined with dampened cheesecloth into another pot, pressing the solids to release all of the juices and extract their flavor. Cool the stock and refrigerate for several hours or overnight. When cold, skim of the fat that has risen to the surface. The stock may be refrigerated for up to 3 days, or it may be frozen in freezer bags or other airtight containers for up to 3 months.

Acknowledgments

It is such a pleasure to produce a book with my wonderful editor Elaine Maisner, and to be published by the University of North Carolina Press. My eagle-eyed copyeditor, Mary Carley Caviness, is a lifesaver. They have made my job easier and have made me look smarter than I am.

My friends and colleagues, among them Sheri Castle and Nancie McDermott (the schoolmarm), have provided tremendous support. My husband, Cliff, is not only a great tester, but he also does the dishes. I hope he realizes how integral a part of my cookbook team he really is. My daughter, Rachel, has been a wonderful taste-tester—I'm so glad she loves chicken!

Friends from far and wide contributed in so many ways—whether with chicken discussions or sharing a recipe. Stephanie Delany, Nathalie Dupree, Patrick Evans-Hylton, Asha Gomez, Kellie Wood Meckes, Andrea Pell, Michael Phillips, Toni Tipton-Martin, and so many others are all part of this story.

Index